HOW THE U.S. ELECTION SYSTEM WORKS

Did You Know Series

CONTENTS

INTRODUCTION.

The United States plays a highly influential role in world politics today, shaped by its military power, economic strength, diplomatic presence, and leadership in international institutions. Here's a breakdown of the key areas where the U.S. exerts influence in global affairs:

1. Global Superpower Status

The U.S. is considered a global superpower, largely due to its unmatched military capabilities. It has the largest defense budget in the world and maintains military bases in over 70 countries. This extensive military presence allows the U.S. to project power and influence international security decisions. Its role in NATO and other defense pacts, like the U.S.-Japan and U.S.-South Korea alliances, underpins its centrality in global security architecture.

In areas like the Indo-Pacific and Europe, the U.S. serves as a counterbalance to rising powers such as China and assertive actors like Russia. This geopolitical influence is evident in its support for Ukraine against Russian aggression and its involvement in ensuring freedom of navigation in contested waters, such as the South China Sea.

2. Economic Influence

The U.S. economy, the largest in the world, plays a dominant role in global trade, finance, and economic policy. The U.S. dollar is the world's primary reserve currency, used in global trade and held by central banks worldwide. This gives the U.S. considerable leverage over global economic stability and the ability to influence international economic norms through institutions like the International Monetary Fund (IMF) and the World Bank, which are headquartered in the U.S.

Additionally, U.S. economic policies, including decisions on trade tariffs, sanctions, and foreign aid, can significantly impact other nations. For example, U.S.-China trade tensions affect global markets, while sanctions imposed by the U.S. on countries like Iran, North Korea, and Russia have global geopolitical and economic consequences.

3. Leadership in International Organizations

The U.S. plays a leading role in shaping the policies and decisions of key international organizations, including the United Nations (UN), World Trade Organization (WTO), and NATO. The U.S. is a founding member and major funder of these institutions, giving it significant sway over international diplomatic and peacekeeping initiatives.

At the UN, the U.S. holds a permanent seat on the Security Council, allowing it to veto resolutions and shape decisions on international security matters. The U.S. has also been instrumental in global responses to crises like the COVID-19 pandemic, humanitarian aid in conflict zones, and environmental initiatives such as the Paris Climate Agreement, even though it has faced criticism for temporarily withdrawing from the latter under the Trump administration.

4. Diplomatic Influence and Soft Power

The U.S. leverages its diplomatic network to influence political outcomes worldwide. It engages in diplomacy on key issues like nuclear non-proliferation, conflict resolution, and human rights advocacy. U.S. diplomacy is often involved in negotiations, such as the Iran Nuclear Deal (JCPOA) and peace efforts in the Middle East, including Israeli-Palestinian negotiations.

Beyond hard power, the U.S. exercises considerable soft power through its cultural, educational, and technological exports. Hollywood, Silicon Valley, and American universities are global leaders in shaping cultural norms, technological innovations, and educational standards. U.S. media, entertainment, and technology companies like Google, Apple, and Facebook also have global reach, influencing digital spaces, communication, and culture.

5. Role in Addressing Global Challenges

The U.S. plays a central role in addressing transnational challenges such as climate change, terrorism, global pandemics, and international trade disputes. U.S. involvement in global initiatives like the Paris Agreement signals its critical role in international environmental diplomacy. Although the U.S. briefly exited the agreement under the Trump administration, its re-entry under the Biden administration marked a renewed commitment to global climate leadership.

In combating terrorism, the U.S. has led coalitions against groups like ISIS and Al-Qaeda, playing a prominent role in shaping international counterterrorism strategies. The U.S. also leads in humanitarian and development aid, providing assistance in response to natural disasters, famines, and conflict.

6. Competition with China and Russia

In the current global order, the U.S. faces increasing competition from China and Russia.

Both countries challenge U.S. influence in different regions and global institutions. China's growing economic power, military expansion, and efforts to lead global initiatives like the Belt and Road Initiative (BRI) pose a direct challenge to U.S. economic and geopolitical interests.

Similarly, Russia's actions in Ukraine, Syria, and its attempts to destabilize Western democracies through cyber-attacks and disinformation campaigns reflect a strategic effort to undermine U.S. influence, particularly in Europe.

The U.S. response to these challenges has involved strengthening alliances, particularly in NATO and the Indo-Pacific (through initiatives like AUKUS and the Quad partnership with Japan, India, and Australia), and promoting free and open international norms that contrast with China's more authoritarian model.

7. Human Rights and Democratic Values

The U.S. has historically positioned itself as a champion of human rights and democracy, although its record is sometimes viewed as inconsistent. The promotion of democratic governance, free elections, and human rights is central to U.S. foreign policy, with programs to support civil society and democratic institutions in regions ranging from Latin America to Africa and Eastern Europe.

U.S. efforts to promote democracy are evident in its support for opposition groups in Venezuela, its stance against military coups, such as in Myanmar, and its advocacy for human rights, such as condemning China's treatment of Uyghur Muslims in Xinjiang. However, U.S. foreign policy has also been criticized for aligning with authoritarian regimes when strategic interests outweigh democratic values, as seen in its relationships with countries like Saudi Arabia.

8. International Trade and Sanctions

The U.S. is a major player in international trade negotiations and has significant influence over global economic policies through its participation in organizations like the WTO. U.S. trade policies can set global standards for issues like intellectual property, labor rights, and environmental regulations.

Sanctions are another tool the U.S. uses to influence global politics. The U.S. has imposed economic sanctions on countries like Russia, Iran, North Korea, and Venezuela to pressure these nations to change their behavior. Sanctions have a profound impact not only on the targeted nations but also on global trade and international relations.

In today's world, the U.S. remains a pivotal actor in shaping international relations and global politics. Its influence is multifaceted, extending through military power, economic leadership, diplomacy, and soft power. However, the U.S. faces significant challenges from emerging powers like China and resurgent rivals like Russia, as well as from internal debates over its role in the world. Despite these challenges, the U.S. continues to play a leading role in addressing global issues, from climate change and terrorism to trade and human rights. As the international landscape evolves, the nature of U.S. influence will likely adapt, but its central position in world politics seems set to endure for the foreseeable future. Who sits in the White House remains significant to the whole world.

CHAPTER 1.

The Basic Structure of the U.S. Government

The U.S. government is one of the most well-known examples of a federal system of governance in the world. This system, which is based on the principles laid out in the U.S. Constitution, divides power between a national government and individual state governments. Its structure is designed to balance power and prevent any single entity from becoming too dominant, thus protecting democracy and ensuring a system of checks and balances. To better understand the U.S. government's framework, it's essential to break down its core components: federalism, the three branches of government (executive, legislative, and judicial), and the relationship between the federal government and state governments.

1. Federalism: The Division of Power

At the heart of the U.S. government's structure is the concept of federalism, a system where power is shared between two levels of government: the federal government and the governments of the 50 individual states. This division of power is meant to allow the federal government to handle matters of national concern, such as defense and foreign policy, while state governments retain authority over more localized issues like education and public safety.

Powers of the Federal Government

The powers of the federal government are outlined in the U.S. Constitution, primarily under Article I, Section 8, which lists specific authorities known as enumerated powers. These powers include the ability to:

- Levy taxes.
- Regulate interstate and international commerce.
- Coin money.
- Maintain armed forces.
- Declare war.
- Establish a postal system.
- Make treaties with foreign countries.

The federal government also has implied powers, derived from the Necessary and Proper Clause (often referred to as the Elastic Clause), which allows Congress to pass laws required to carry out its enumerated powers.

Powers of State Governments

Under the Tenth Amendment to the Constitution, powers not delegated to the federal government nor prohibited to the states are reserved for state governments. These are known as reserved powers and include:

- Administering local governments.
- Regulating education.
- Managing public health and safety.
- Overseeing elections.
- Handling issues like marriage laws and transportation within state boundaries.

Concurrent Powers

There are also concurrent powers, which are shared by both the federal and state governments. These include the power to tax, build roads, and create lower courts.

2. The Three Branches of Government

The U.S. Constitution divides the federal government into three distinct branches: the Executive Branch, the Legislative Branch, and the Judicial Branch. This separation of powers is crucial for preventing any single branch from gaining too much authority, thus ensuring a system of checks and balances.

The Executive Branch

The Executive Branch is responsible for enforcing

the laws of the United States and is headed by the President, who serves as both the head of state and head of government. The President is elected every four years through the Electoral College system and can serve a maximum of two terms.

Roles of the President

- Chief Executive: The President is responsible for executing federal laws and overseeing the federal bureaucracy.
- Commander-in-Chief: The President leads the armed forces and makes critical military decisions.
- Chief Diplomat: The President directs foreign policy, negotiates treaties (with Senate approval), and represents the U.S. internationally.
- Legislative Leader: While not part of the Legislative Branch, the President influences lawmaking by proposing legislation, issuing executive orders, and signing or vetoing bills passed by Congress.
- Chief of State: The President fulfills ceremonial duties and acts as a symbol of national unity.

Executive Departments and Agencies

The President is supported by the Vice President, the Cabinet, and numerous federal agencies. The Cabinet is composed of the heads of 15 executive departments (e.g., the Department of State, Department of Defense, Department of Education) that manage specific areas of national policy. The President also oversees independent agencies like the Environmental Protection

Agency (EPA) and the Central Intelligence Agency (CIA), which play critical roles in implementing federal policies.

The Legislative Branch

The Legislative Branch is tasked with making laws and is composed of Congress, which is a bicameral legislature, meaning it has two separate chambers: the Senate and the House of Representatives.

The Senate

- The Senate has 100 members, with each of the 50 states electing two senators. Senators serve six-year terms, and elections are staggered so that one-third of the Senate is up for election every two years.
- The Senate has unique powers, such as ratifying treaties and confirming presidential appointments to the judiciary and executive branch (e.g., Supreme Court justices, Cabinet members).

The House of Representatives

- The House of Representatives has 435 members, with each state's representation based on its population. Representatives serve two-year terms, and all members are up for election every two years.
- The House holds the power of the purse, meaning it initiates revenue bills, and it also has the authority to impeach federal officials, including the President.

Lawmaking Process

To pass a law, both chambers of Congress must approve the same bill by a majority vote. The bill is then sent to the President, who can either sign it into law or veto it. If the President vetoes the bill, Congress can override the veto with a two-thirds vote in both chambers.

The Judicial Branch

The Judicial Branch is responsible for interpreting laws and determining their constitutionality. It consists of a system of federal courts, with the Supreme Court being the highest court in the land.

The Supreme Court

- The Supreme Court has nine justices, including one Chief Justice. These justices are nominated by the President and confirmed by the Senate, and they serve for life unless they resign, retire, or are impeached.
- The primary role of the Supreme Court is judicial review, the process of determining whether laws or executive actions are constitutional. This power was established by the landmark case Marbury v. Madison in 1803.

Lower Courts

Beneath the Supreme Court are two other levels of federal courts: Courts of Appeals (or circuit courts) and District Courts. District Courts are the trial courts of the federal system, where most cases begin. If a party is dissatisfied with the outcome in a District Court, they may appeal to a Court of Appeals. The Supreme Court hears cases from the Courts of Appeals or state supreme courts when there are significant constitutional questions or national legal importance.

3. Checks and Balances

One of the defining features of the U.S. government system is checks and balances, which ensures that no one branch becomes too powerful. Each branch has the ability to limit the actions of the others in various ways:

- Presidential Veto: The President can veto legislation passed by Congress, but Congress can override the veto with a two-thirds majority in both houses.
- Congressional Oversight: Congress can refuse to approve presidential appointments and treaties. It also has the power to impeach and remove the President and other federal officials.
- Judicial Review: The courts can declare laws or executive actions unconstitutional.
- Appointment Power: The President appoints federal judges, but those appointments must be confirmed by the Senate.

This system creates a balance of power, ensuring that decisions are made with deliberation and consensus, rather than by a single authority.

4. The Relationship Between Federal and State Governments

The Tenth Amendment of the Constitution gives

states significant autonomy, allowing them to govern within their borders as long as they don't violate federal laws or the Constitution. However, conflicts sometimes arise between state and federal law, often leading to court cases that determine which level of government has jurisdiction over a particular issue.

For example, issues like education, policing, and transportation are primarily handled at the state level, while issues like national defense, foreign policy, and interstate commerce are managed by the federal government. Some powers overlap, such as taxation and law enforcement, which are shared by both levels of government.

Federal Preemption

In cases where federal law conflicts with state law, federal law generally takes precedence. This is known as federal preemption and is based on the Supremacy Clause of the Constitution.

Conclusion

The U.S. government's structure is a complex system of federalism, separation of powers, and checks and balances, all designed to protect democracy and prevent the concentration of power. Each branch of government—executive, legislative, and judicial—plays a distinct yet interconnected role in governing the country, ensuring that the rule of law prevails and that no single institution or individual wields unchecked authority. This system has allowed the U.S. to maintain stability and democratic governance for more than two centuries, serving as a model for many other nations worldwide.

CHAPTER 2.

Types of Elections in the United States

The U.S. electoral system is a dynamic and multi-layered process designed to accommodate the country's federal structure and democratic ideals. Elections in the United States are held at various levels—federal, state, and local—and occur for a range of offices, from the President of the United States to local school board members. The system ensures that citizens have a say in their governance and helps maintain a representative democracy. In this chapter, we will explore the different types of elections in the U.S., including presidential, congressional, state, and local elections, as well as primary and general elections, special elections, and the electoral processes used in referendums and initiatives.

1. Presidential Elections

The Presidential Election is perhaps the most high-profile election in the United States. It is held every four years on the first Tuesday after the first Monday in November. The election determines who will serve as the President and Vice President of the United States for the next four-year term.

Electoral Process

The U.S. does not elect its President by a direct national popular vote. Instead, it uses a system known as the Electoral College. Here's how it works:

- Electoral College: Each state is allocated a number of electors based on its representation in Congress (the total number of senators and representatives). In total, there are 538 electors, and a candidate must win a majority —270 electoral votes—to become President.
- Winner-takes-all system: In most states, the candidate who wins the most votes in that state receives all of its electoral votes. Only two states, Maine and Nebraska, use a proportional system where electoral votes can be split between candidates.

Primaries and Caucuses

Before the general election, political parties in the U.S. hold primary elections and caucuses to choose their nominees for President.

- Primaries: These are statewide elections where party members vote for their preferred candidate. There are two main types: closed primaries, where only registered party members can vote, and open primaries, where any voter, regardless of party affiliation, can participate.

- Caucuses: These are meetings where party members gather to discuss and vote for their preferred candidate. Caucuses are less common but are still used in some states like Iowa.

After the primaries and caucuses, the parties hold national conventions, where they formally nominate their candidate for President. This candidate then selects a Vice Presidential running mate, and together they campaign in the general election.

General Election

The general election is where voters across the country cast their votes for President. While the popular vote is important, the real determinant is the Electoral College, which formally elects the President in December. If no candidate receives a majority of electoral votes, the election is decided by the House of Representatives, where each state delegation casts one vote to elect the President.

2. Congressional Elections

In addition to the presidential election, the U.S. holds congressional elections every two years. These elections decide who will represent the people in the U.S. Congress, which consists of two chambers: the Senate and the House of

Representatives.

Senate Elections

- Number of Senators: Each state has two senators, regardless of population, meaning there are 100 senators in total.
- Term Length: Senators serve six-year terms, but elections are staggered so that only one-third of the Senate is up for election every two years.
- Election Process: Senators are elected in statewide elections, and the winner is decided by a simple majority of the popular vote.

House of Representatives Elections

- Number of Representatives: The House of Representatives has 435 members, with each state's representation based on its population. States with larger populations, like California and Texas, have more representatives, while smaller states like Wyoming and Vermont have only one.
- Term Length: Representatives serve two-year terms, and all 435 seats are up for election every two years.
- Election Process: House members are elected from congressional districts within their states. These districts are drawn based on population data from the U.S. Census, which is conducted every ten years.

3. State and Local Elections

The U.S. is a federal republic, meaning that state governments operate independently from the federal government in many respects. State and local elections are held to choose governors, state legislators, mayors, and other local officials.

These elections vary widely depending on the state and locality, but they follow general patterns similar to federal elections.

Gubernatorial Elections

- Governor's Role: The governor is the chief executive of a state and has powers similar to those of the President but at the state level, such as signing or vetoing bills, overseeing the state's budget, and commanding the state's National Guard.
- Term Length: Governors typically serve four-year terms, though some states, like New Hampshire and Vermont, have two-year terms.
- Election Process: Like presidential elections, gubernatorial elections are often held every four years, and most states elect their governors in midterm election years, halfway through the President's term.

State Legislatures

- Bicameral System: Most states have bicameral legislatures similar to Congress, consisting of a Senate and a House of Representatives or Assembly. Only Nebraska has a unicameral, or one-house, legislature.
- Term Length: State senators and representatives serve terms that vary by state but are usually two or four years.
- Election Process: State legislators are elected from districts within the state, and elections can be held in even-numbered or odd-numbered years, depending on the state.

Local Elections

Local elections select officials for cities, towns, counties, and other municipalities. Positions may

include:

- Mayors: Elected as the executive head of a city or town.
- City Council Members: Serve as the legislative body of a city.
- Sheriffs: Elected law enforcement officers in some counties.
- School Board Members: Oversee local education policies and budgets.

Local elections can vary significantly in timing and procedures across different states and municipalities. Many are held in odd-numbered years or in conjunction with state or federal elections.

4. Primary Elections

Primary elections are a key part of the U.S. electoral process. They are held to select candidates who will represent their political parties in the general election. The two major political parties in the U.S., the Democratic Party and the Republican Party, use primaries to determine their nominees for various offices.

Types of Primaries

- Closed Primaries: Only registered members of a particular party can vote in that party's primary.
- Open Primaries: Any registered voter can participate in any party's primary, regardless of their own party affiliation.
- Semi-Closed Primaries: Unaffiliated voters can choose which party's primary to vote in, but voters

registered with a party can only vote in their party's primary.

In addition to primaries for presidential candidates, primaries are also held for congressional, state, and local offices.

5. Special Elections

Special elections are held to fill vacancies that arise when an officeholder dies, resigns, or is removed from office before the end of their term. Special elections can be held at the federal, state, or local level.

For example, if a U.S. senator leaves office mid-term, the state may hold a special election to choose a replacement. Special elections may also be called for state legislatures, governors, or local offices. These elections are generally held on dates separate from regular elections.

6. Referendums and Initiatives

In addition to electing officials, voters in the U.S. can directly participate in the legislative process through referendums and initiatives, which allow them to approve or reject laws or propose new laws.

Referendums

- A referendum is a direct vote in which citizens decide whether to approve or reject a law passed by the legislature.

- Mandatory Referendums: Some laws, especially those related to constitutional amendments or bond measures, require voter approval before taking effect.
- Optional Referendums: Voters can sometimes petition to have a law placed on the ballot for approval or rejection after it has been passed by the legislature.

Initiatives

- An initiative allows voters to propose new laws or amendments to the state constitution. Citizens gather signatures to place an initiative on the ballot, and then voters decide whether to approve it.
- Direct Initiatives: If the required number of signatures is collected, the proposal goes directly on the ballot for a vote.
- Indirect Initiatives: The proposal goes to the state legislature first, and if it is not passed, it may then be placed on the ballot for a public vote.

Referendums and initiatives are more common at the state and local levels, particularly in states like California, where the initiative process has played a major role in shaping public policy.

Conclusion

The U.S. electoral system is both complex and inclusive, offering numerous avenues for citizens to participate in governance. Presidential, congressional, state, and local elections provide the foundation for representative democracy, while primary elections, special elections, and mechanisms like referendums and initiatives ensure that citizens have a direct say in the political process. Although the specifics of each type of election vary, they all work together to create a system in which power ultimately rests with the people. This diverse and multi-tiered election process reflects the federal structure of the United States and reinforces the democratic values on which the country was founded.

The Role of Preliminary Presidential Campaigns and National Televised Debates in U.S. Elections

As we have mentioned, Presidential elections in the United States are multi-stage, complex processes that extend beyond the voting booths on Election Day. Two critical phases in this process are the preliminary presidential campaigns and the national televised debates. Both play crucial roles in shaping the final election outcome, influencing voter perceptions, determining candidate viability, and steering the public discourse. The preliminary campaign period helps define the field of candidates, while national televised debates offer a unique platform for candidates to present themselves to the American public, contrast their policies, and demonstrate leadership qualities.

We will explore the roles that these stages of the U.S. presidential election process play in shaping the final vote, focusing on the preliminary campaigns, their impact on candidates and voters, and the significance of national televised debates.

1. The Preliminary Presidential Campaign

The preliminary presidential campaign, often referred to as the primary campaign, begins well before the general election. This phase occurs during the lead-up to party primaries and caucuses and serves to identify, refine, and promote candidates within each political party. It is during this period that potential nominees begin to announce their candidacy, raise funds, and lay the groundwork for their campaigns by establishing their platforms and building voter support.

Early Candidate Announcements and Strategy

The preliminary campaign starts with candidates formally announcing their intention to run for President, usually a year or more before the general election. Announcing early provides several advantages:

- Building Name Recognition: For lesser-known candidates, an early announcement allows them to begin building name recognition and establishing their identity in a crowded field. This is particularly important for candidates running against high-profile figures.
- Fundraising and Campaign Infrastructure:

Fundraising is a crucial element of U.S. elections, and early announcements allow candidates to tap into donor networks and build campaign infrastructure, including staff, advertising, and outreach operations.

• Shaping Public Perception: Early in the race, candidates have the opportunity to define themselves before their opponents or the media can do so. This allows them to frame their own narrative, policies, and qualifications.

Voter Engagement and Policy Formulation

The preliminary campaign is not only important for the candidates but also for the electorate. During this period, voters begin to familiarize themselves with the various candidates and their positions on key issues. It is a critical time for candidates to lay out their platforms on topics like healthcare, the economy, foreign policy, and immigration. The Iowa Caucus and New Hampshire Primary, as the first contests in the primary season, are often seen as bellwethers that can make or break a candidacy by testing a candidate's appeal and organizational strength.

Candidates travel across the country, participating in town halls, rallies, and smaller meet-and-greets to build a coalition of supporters. These efforts allow candidates to:

• Gauge Public Sentiment: By interacting with voters, candidates can refine their platforms based on what resonates most with the electorate. For instance, a candidate may start with a focus on foreign policy but shift emphasis to healthcare if it proves more pressing to voters.

- Test Campaign Messages: The preliminary campaign is a laboratory for candidates to test their slogans, rhetoric, and policy proposals before a smaller, engaged electorate. It allows them to find what messages work best and where adjustments may be necessary.

The Importance of Polls and Media Coverage

During the preliminary campaign, public opinion polls and media coverage play significant roles in shaping the narrative around candidates. Candidates with higher polling numbers typically attract more media attention, which can further enhance their visibility and credibility with voters. On the flip side, poor polling results can lead to negative media coverage, making it harder for a candidate to gain traction.

The media serves as both an amplifier and a filter during this stage. While it can help promising candidates gain national attention, it also scrutinizes candidates intensely, examining their past records, policy positions, and even personal histories. In many ways, the preliminary campaign functions as a vetting process, helping to winnow down the field to the most viable contenders.

2. National Televised Debates: A Platform for Public Scrutiny

The national televised debates are pivotal

moments in both the primary and general election campaigns. They offer voters a direct comparison between the candidates, giving them the chance to hear candidates' positions on issues, evaluate their demeanor, and observe how they perform under pressure.

Debates During the Primary Campaign

During the primary season, televised debates are held between the candidates competing for their party's nomination. These debates serve several purposes:

- Vetting Candidates in a Public Forum: Primary debates give voters a chance to see candidates engage with each other on key issues. They are a test of candidates' ability to defend their platforms, articulate policy solutions, and challenge their opponents in a high-pressure environment.
- Creating Defining Moments: Debates often produce memorable moments—whether a candidate delivers a powerful line, stumbles on an answer, or is attacked by an opponent—that can shift the dynamics of the race. For example, a candidate who performs poorly in a debate may see a sharp drop in support, while a strong performance can catapult a candidate into the spotlight.
- Revealing Policy Depth: Voters can gauge the depth of a candidate's knowledge on specific issues during these debates. A candidate's ability to discuss complex policy matters clearly and confidently can significantly impact their perception as presidential material.

In the primary debates, candidates often focus on drawing distinctions between themselves and their fellow party members, highlighting differences in their platforms. The debates also offer lower-polling candidates a chance to elevate their profile if they perform well against more established competitors.

Debates in the General Election

Once the nominees from each party have been selected, the national televised debates between the major-party candidates become some of the most-watched political events in the election cycle. These debates typically occur in the fall, close to Election Day, and have a significant impact on undecided voters.

The Commission on Presidential Debates (CPD) organizes these events, which usually consist of three presidential debates and one vice-presidential debate. The format may vary, with some debates featuring direct questioning by moderators and others allowing voters to ask questions in a town hall-style setting.

The Role of Debates in the General Election

The general election debates are crucial for several reasons:

- Reaching a National Audience: Debates allow candidates to address tens of millions of voters simultaneously, offering a direct, unfiltered view of their policies and personalities. The audience includes undecided voters, who often play a critical role in deciding the outcome of the election.

• Shaping Public Perception: For many voters, the debates are the first and only time they see the candidates directly interacting with each other. The candidates' composure, ability to handle tough questions, and responses to their opponents can significantly affect their standing with the public. A strong or weak debate performance can change the momentum of the campaign.

• Focusing on Key Issues: Debates highlight the most important issues of the election, providing candidates the opportunity to outline their plans and argue why their policies are better for the country. This format also forces candidates to discuss their policies in greater detail, which can clarify their positions for voters.

Debate Impact on the Election Outcome

Debates have a history of affecting election outcomes. For example, the 1960 Kennedy-Nixon debates were the first-ever televised presidential debates and are widely credited with helping John F. Kennedy win the election. His charismatic presence and calm demeanor contrasted sharply with Richard Nixon's tired appearance, influencing millions of viewers.

More recently, debates have played a critical role in shifting perceptions, as in the case of Barack Obama versus Mitt Romney in 2012, when Romney's strong performance in the first debate narrowed the polling gap between him and the incumbent. While debates rarely decide elections on their own, they can reinforce or weaken voter preferences, especially among undecided voters.

3. The Interplay Between Preliminary Campaigns and Debates

The preliminary campaign and national debates are interconnected phases that together shape the final election outcome. The preliminary campaign serves as a proving ground, where candidates build their credibility, hone their messages, and prepare for the national stage. By the time candidates reach the general election debates, they have been through months, if not years, of campaigning, refining their arguments and learning how to handle the intense scrutiny of a nationwide audience.

Debates build on the groundwork laid during the preliminary campaign by offering a final test of the candidates' policies and personas. For voters who have been following the campaigns, debates can reaffirm their choices or cause them to reconsider. For less engaged voters, debates may serve as their primary means of evaluating the candidates before casting their ballots.

Conclusion

The preliminary presidential campaigns and national televised debates are essential components of the U.S. electoral process. Together, they provide a structure for evaluating candidates, refining voter preferences, and shaping the final election outcome. The preliminary campaigns allow candidates to introduce themselves, develop their platforms, and build a base of support, while the national debates give them an opportunity to present their ideas on a national stage and test their ability to lead under pressure. Both stages ensure that voters are informed and that the candidates who make it to the general election have been thoroughly vetted, making these elements indispensable to the democratic process.

CHAPTER 3.

Who Can Vote in the United States?

Voting is one of the most fundamental rights in a democracy, allowing citizens to participate in the decision-making process of their government. In the United States, the right to vote has evolved over centuries and is governed by a combination of federal, state, and local laws. While voting rights are widely protected today, historically, many groups were excluded from the electorate. Even now, the rules about who can vote vary slightly from state to state, influenced by factors like age, residency, citizenship, and criminal history.

In this essay, we will explore who can vote in the United States by examining the basic qualifications for voting, the historical evolution of voting rights, current restrictions, and the ongoing debates about expanding or restricting access to the ballot.

1. Basic Qualifications for Voting

In the United States, the right to vote is a privilege granted to citizens, and there are several basic qualifications that individuals must meet in order to be eligible to vote.

A. Citizenship

To vote in federal, state, or local elections, an individual must be a U.S. citizen. U.S. citizenship can be acquired in one of two ways:

- Birthright Citizenship: People born in the U.S. or born abroad to U.S. citizens are automatically citizens under the 14th Amendment to the Constitution.
- Naturalization: Immigrants who move to the U.S. and become legal permanent residents (Green Card holders) can apply for citizenship through the naturalization process, which includes passing a civics test, demonstrating English proficiency, and meeting residency requirements.

Only U.S. citizens are allowed to vote in federal elections. Some states and localities have experimented with allowing non-citizens to vote in specific local elections, but this is extremely rare and controversial.

B. Age

The minimum age to vote in U.S. elections is 18 years old, a right established by the 26th Amendment in 1971. Prior to this amendment, the voting age in most states was 21. The change to 18 was driven by the argument that if 18-year-olds were old enough to be drafted into military service during the Vietnam War, they should also be able to vote.

Some states allow individuals who are 17 years old to vote in primary elections if they will turn 18 by the time of the general election. However, this varies by state and is not universally applied.

C. Residency

To vote in a U.S. election, an individual must be a resident of the state and district in which they are voting. Residency requirements vary by state, but generally, a person must live in their state for a certain amount of time before being eligible to register to vote. This period can range from 10 to 30 days, depending on the state.

Residency rules ensure that voters are casting ballots in the jurisdiction where they live, which affects local representation and policies. Temporary residents, such as college students or military personnel, may face special rules about where they can vote, depending on whether they intend to maintain their permanent residency elsewhere.

D. Voter Registration

To vote in most U.S. elections, eligible citizens

must first register to vote. Voter registration processes vary by state, but generally, individuals can register in person, by mail, or online. Some states allow for same-day voter registration, where citizens can register and vote on the same day, while others have registration deadlines that occur several weeks before an election.

2. Historical Evolution of Voting Rights

The right to vote in the U.S. has undergone significant changes over the centuries, expanding from a narrow group of white, male property owners to include almost all adult citizens. This expansion has been shaped by social movements, legal battles, and constitutional amendments.

A. Early Voting Restrictions

When the U.S. was founded, voting was largely restricted to white male property owners. Each state set its own qualifications, but the common practice was to limit suffrage to those who held property, believing that only property owners had a vested interest in the governance of the country.

B. The 15th Amendment and the End of Racial Exclusions

After the Civil War, the 15th Amendment (ratified in 1870) granted African American men the right to vote, stating that the right to vote could not be denied on the basis of "race, color, or previous condition of servitude." However, despite this constitutional protection, many Southern states implemented discriminatory practices such as poll taxes, literacy tests, and grandfather clauses to prevent African Americans from voting. These tactics were part of Jim Crow laws, which upheld racial segregation and disenfranchisement for nearly a century.

C. Women's Suffrage and the 19th Amendment

Women in the U.S. fought for decades for the right to vote through the women's suffrage movement. In 1920, the 19th Amendment was ratified, granting women the right to vote nationwide. Before this amendment, some states, particularly in the West, had already granted women limited suffrage rights.

D. The Voting Rights Act of 1965

One of the most significant advancements in voting rights came with the passage of the Voting Rights Act of 1965. This landmark legislation was designed to eliminate racial discrimination in voting, particularly in Southern states where African Americans had been systematically disenfranchised. The Act banned literacy tests, provided federal oversight of voter registration in areas with a history of discrimination, and allowed the federal government to investigate and prosecute voting rights violations.

E. The 26th Amendment and Youth Voting

As mentioned earlier, the 26th Amendment lowered the voting age from 21 to 18, broadening the electorate to include younger citizens. The change was partly motivated by youth activism during the 1960s and 1970s, especially around the Vietnam War.

3. Current Restrictions on Voting Rights

While the right to vote is broadly protected in the United States, there are still some restrictions that prevent certain groups from voting. These restrictions can vary by state and often become points of contention in political and legal debates.

A. Felon Disenfranchisement

One of the most significant current voting restrictions involves individuals with felony convictions. Most states impose some form of felon disenfranchisement, though the rules vary widely:

- Maine and Vermont are the only states that allow felons to vote even while incarcerated.
- Other states allow individuals to vote once they have completed their prison sentences, parole, or probation.

- In some states, especially in the South, individuals with felony convictions are permanently disenfranchised unless they receive a pardon from the governor or another official.

The issue of felon disenfranchisement has sparked debates about civil rights, with advocates arguing that denying formerly incarcerated individuals the right to vote undermines their rehabilitation and reintegration into society.

B. Voter ID Laws

In recent years, many states have passed laws requiring voters to show photo identification at the polls. Proponents argue that these laws prevent voter fraud, but opponents argue that they disproportionately impact marginalized groups, such as low-income individuals, racial minorities, and the elderly, who may be less likely to possess valid identification.

Voter ID laws vary widely in terms of the types of ID accepted and whether voters can cast provisional ballots if they do not have ID. Critics argue that such laws amount to voter suppression, while supporters see them as a common-sense safeguard.

C. Residency and Citizenship Laws

Non-citizens, including legal permanent residents (Green Card holders), cannot vote in federal elections. Some cities, like San Francisco, have experimented with allowing non-citizens to vote in certain local elections, such as school board races, but such initiatives are rare and often controversial. Similarly, individuals who move between states or have temporary residencies may face challenges meeting residency requirements, though most states provide ways for military members and other citizens abroad to vote by absentee ballot.

4. Efforts to Expand Voting Access

In contrast to the restrictions on voting, there are ongoing efforts to expand access to the ballot. These efforts aim to ensure that more people are able to exercise their right to vote and that barriers to voting are minimized.

A. Automatic and Same-Day Voter Registration

One of the most significant trends in expanding voting access is the push for automatic voter registration (AVR). AVR automatically registers eligible citizens to vote when they interact with certain government agencies, such as the Department of Motor Vehicles. States like California and Oregon have implemented AVR, leading to significant increases in voter registration.

Similarly, same-day voter registration allows

individuals to register and vote on the same day, which can help increase voter turnout, particularly among younger and more mobile populations.

B. Mail-In and Early Voting

Expanding access to mail-in voting and early voting options is another key focus for voting rights advocates. Many states now allow any voter to request a mail-in ballot, while others require an excuse, such as illness or being out of the country, to vote by mail. Additionally, early voting periods, which allow citizens to vote in person before Election Day, have become common, giving people more flexibility in when they vote.

Conclusion

The right to vote in the United States is a cornerstone of democratic participation, but it has been shaped by centuries of legal, political, and social developments. Today, most U.S. citizens aged 18 and older can vote, but restrictions still exist based on factors like felony convictions and identification requirements. Despite these challenges, efforts to expand voting access continue, ensuring that as many citizens as possible have the opportunity to participate in elections. Voting remains both a right and a responsibility, central to the functioning of democracy in the United States.

CHAPTER 4.

The Two Major Political Parties

The Historical Development of the Two Major Political Parties in the United States

The United States' political system has long been dominated by two major political parties: the Democratic Party and the Republican Party. These two parties have shaped American politics for well over a century, but their ideologies, platforms, and constituencies have evolved significantly since their inception. Understanding the historical development of these two political parties offers insight into how they have become the pillars of U.S. democracy and how their shifting identities reflect broader societal changes in America.

This essay will provide a background on the two-party system, trace the historical development of both the Democratic and Republican parties, and examine the key events that have shaped their modern ideologies and political strategies.

1. Background on the Two-Party System in the U.S.

The two-party system in the United States has become a defining feature of its political landscape, despite the absence of any constitutional requirement for political parties. The founders of the United States were, in fact, skeptical of political parties, fearing they would lead to division and factionalism. In Federalist No. 10, James Madison famously warned of the dangers of factions, while George Washington, in his Farewell Address, cautioned against the "baneful effects" of political parties.

Nevertheless, political parties began to emerge almost immediately after the nation's founding as different factions coalesced around key issues, particularly the size and scope of the federal government. Over time, the U.S. political system has solidified into a two-party structure, primarily due to the "first-past-the-post" electoral system, where the candidate with the most votes wins. This system tends to favor two dominant parties, as smaller parties often struggle to gain traction in winner-take-all elections.

Historically, the two-party system in the U.S. has undergone several party realignments, where the dominant parties have shifted their platforms, ideologies, and core constituencies. The modern Democratic and Republican parties are the latest iterations in this evolution.

2. The Democratic Party: From Jeffersonian Democracy to Modern Progressivism

A. Origins and Early History (1790s-1820s)

The roots of the Democratic Party trace back to the late 18th century, with the formation of the Democratic-Republican Party, also known as the Jeffersonian Republicans. This party was founded by Thomas Jefferson and James Madison in opposition to the Federalist Party, led by Alexander Hamilton and John Adams. The central ideological divide between the two parties revolved around the power of the federal government. The Democratic-Republicans favored limited federal government, strict constitutional interpretation, and greater power for individual states, reflecting a strong commitment to agrarianism and a suspicion of centralized economic power.

The Democratic-Republicans dominated U.S. politics after the decline of the Federalist Party in the early 1800s, but by the 1820s, internal divisions within the party led to the formation of two new factions: Andrew Jackson's populist Democrats and the National Republicans led by John Quincy Adams and Henry Clay. This split marked the birth of the modern Democratic Party, officially founded in 1828 with Jackson's election to the presidency.

B. The Jacksonian Era and the Growth of Democracy (1828-1850s)

The Democratic Party under Andrew Jackson embraced a populist and egalitarian ethos, positioning itself as the party of the "common man." Jackson's presidency emphasized democratic expansion, particularly by advocating for the elimination of property qualifications for voting, which significantly expanded suffrage to all white men. The party also opposed the Second Bank of the United States, which Jackson viewed as an institution that favored wealthy elites at the expense of ordinary citizens.

During this period, the Democratic Party's platform centered on the following key principles:

• States' Rights: A commitment to limiting federal government power and advocating for the sovereignty of individual states.

• Westward Expansion: Support for Manifest Destiny and the expansion of U.S. territory, though this often led to conflicts over slavery in new states.

• Pro-Slavery Stance: Southern Democrats, in particular, were staunch defenders of slavery, seeing it as integral to the economy and social order of the South.

C. The Civil War and Reconstruction (1860s-1870s)

The issue of slavery eventually led to a major political realignment. The Democratic Party split in the 1860 election, with Northern Democrats supporting Stephen Douglas and his policy of popular sovereignty, and Southern Democrats backing John C. Breckinridge, who favored the expansion of slavery into new territories. The split helped Abraham Lincoln, the Republican candidate, win the presidency, leading to the Civil War.

After the war, the Democratic Party became associated with the South and the defense of white supremacy, particularly through its opposition to Reconstruction and efforts to protect the rights of newly freed African Americans. Southern Democrats, known as Dixiecrats, dominated Southern politics, using policies like Jim Crow laws and racial segregation to maintain white control.

D. The Progressive Era and the New Deal (1900s-1930s)

By the early 20th century, the Democratic Party began to shift its ideology, partly in response to the Progressive Movement. Figures like Woodrow Wilson (President from 1913 to 1921) promoted reforms like anti-trust legislation, women's suffrage, and workers' rights, marking the party's gradual embrace of more progressive policies.

However, it was during the presidency of Franklin D. Roosevelt (1933-1945) that the Democratic Party underwent a profound transformation. Roosevelt's New Deal, a series of government programs aimed at alleviating the effects of the Great Depression, marked the Democratic Party's shift toward a more interventionist federal government. The New Deal coalition brought together labor unions, minorities (especially African Americans), urban progressives, and Southern whites, creating a diverse and powerful political base that dominated U.S. politics for much of the mid-20th century.

E. Civil Rights and the Modern Democratic Party (1960s-Present)

The 1960s marked another major realignment within the Democratic Party, particularly with regard to civil rights. Under Presidents John F. Kennedy and Lyndon B. Johnson, the Democratic Party supported landmark civil rights legislation, including the Civil Rights Act of 1964 and the Voting Rights Act of 1965. These policies alienated many Southern white voters, who began shifting toward the Republican Party, but they cemented the Democratic Party's commitment to racial equality and social justice.

The modern Democratic Party is associated with liberal positions on a wide range of issues, including:

- Economic Equality: Advocating for a stronger social safety net, healthcare reform, and progressive taxation.
- Civil Rights: Supporting LGBTQ+ rights, racial equality, and gender equality.
- Environmental Protection: Emphasizing the need for action on climate change and environmental sustainability.

3. The Republican Party: From Anti-Slavery Roots to Conservative Stalwart

A. Origins and Early History (1850s-1870s)

The Republican Party was founded in 1854 in response to the Kansas-Nebraska Act, which allowed for the potential expansion of slavery into new U.S. territories. The party emerged as a coalition of anti-slavery activists, former Whigs, and northern Democrats who opposed the expansion of slavery. It quickly gained momentum as the leading opposition to the Democratic Party, which was seen as pro-slavery.

The Republican Party took a strong moral stance against the spread of slavery, which became the defining issue of the party in its early years. Abraham Lincoln, the party's first successful presidential candidate, was elected in 1860 on a platform of preventing the extension of slavery into new states and territories. His election directly precipitated the Southern states' secession and the outbreak of the Civil War.

B. The Civil War and Reconstruction Era (1860s-1870s)

During the Civil War, the Republican Party became synonymous with the Union's efforts to preserve the nation and abolish slavery. After the war, the party led Reconstruction, a period of political and social change in the South. Republicans supported amendments to the Constitution that abolished slavery (the 13th Amendment), granted citizenship to former slaves (the 14th Amendment), and protected African American voting rights (the 15th

Amendment).

However, after the end of Reconstruction in 1877, the Republican Party's influence in the South waned, and Democrats regained control of Southern politics. The party became more focused on industrial development and big business interests in the North.

C. The Gilded Age and the Progressive Era (1880s-1920s)

In the late 19th and early 20th centuries, the Republican Party became the party of big business and industrialization. It supported protective tariffs, a strong national economy, and limited government intervention in the economy. This era, known as the Gilded Age, saw Republicans align closely with wealthy business interests.

However, during the Progressive Era, some Republicans, like President Theodore Roosevelt, adopted progressive policies aimed at curbing corporate power, protecting consumers, and conserving natural resources. This created a division within the party between conservative Republicans and progressive reformers.

D. The New Deal Opposition and the Conservative Shift (1930s-1960s)

The Great Depression and Franklin D. Roosevelt's New Deal programs saw the Republican Party shift toward opposition to expanded government intervention in the economy. Republicans criticized the New Deal as overreach and advocated for limited government and free-market principles.

After World War II, the Republican Party, particularly under the leadership of Barry Goldwater and later Ronald Reagan, embraced a conservative ideology focused on reducing the size of government, cutting taxes, and opposing communism abroad.

E. The Reagan Revolution and Modern Republicanism (1980s-Present)

The election of Ronald Reagan in 1980 marked a significant turning point for the Republican Party, solidifying its modern conservative platform. Reagan promoted policies of limited government, free-market economics, strong national defense, and traditional social values. His presidency established the GOP as the party of economic conservatism, deregulation, and lower taxes, with a focus on individual responsibility over government welfare programs.

In recent decades, the Republican Party has

further embraced conservative positions on social issues, such as opposing abortion and same-sex marriage, while championing Second Amendment rights and religious freedom. The party's base has also shifted toward a more populist, working-class constituency, especially with the rise of Donald Trump in 2016, whose platform included anti-immigration policies, economic nationalism, and a rejection of establishment politics.

4. Key Differences Between the Modern Democratic and Republican Parties

Today, the Democratic and Republican parties represent starkly different visions for the future of the United States. Some of the key areas of divergence include:

- Size and Role of Government: Democrats tend to support a larger role for government in providing social services, regulating the economy, and addressing issues like healthcare and climate change. Republicans advocate for smaller government, lower taxes, and deregulation to promote free-market solutions.
- Social Issues: Democrats are more likely to support progressive policies on issues like LGBTQ+ rights, racial equality, and abortion rights, while Republicans generally emphasize traditional values, religious freedom, and pro-life positions.
- Economic Policy: Democrats favor progressive taxation and a robust social safety net, while Republicans prioritize tax cuts, reducing government

spending, and promoting economic growth through free enterprise.

- Immigration: Democrats typically advocate for comprehensive immigration reform and a path to citizenship for undocumented immigrants, while Republicans have increasingly focused on border security and limiting immigration.

Conclusion

The development of the Democratic and Republican parties reflects the broader political, social, and economic changes that have shaped the United States over its history. From their origins in debates over the size and power of the federal government to their modern-day ideological divides, these two parties have evolved and adapted to the shifting priorities and values of the American electorate. Despite periodic realignments and internal conflicts, the Democratic and Republican parties remain the dominant forces in U.S. politics, representing contrasting visions of governance, society, and the role of government in citizens' lives. As the country continues to change, so too will the platforms and priorities of these two major political parties.

The two major political parties in the U.S.—the Democratic Party and the Republican Party—have evolved significantly over time, and their current platforms for the 2024 election reflect stark contrasts on key issues. Here's an overview of their views and the two major candidates running for the presidency.

Democratic Party - Key Views for 2024

The Democratic Party's platform for 2024 emphasizes progressivism, with a focus on expanding social protections and civil rights. Key issues include:

- Abortion and Reproductive Rights: The Democratic Party has made abortion rights a defining issue. The platform strongly opposes the Supreme Court's decision to overturn *Roe v. Wade* and pledges to codify abortion rights into federal law. Democrats also want to repeal the Hyde Amendment, which prohibits federal funding for most abortions, and support widespread access to medication abortion.

- Healthcare: Democrats continue to support expanding access to healthcare, building on the Affordable Care Act. The party emphasizes reducing healthcare costs and expanding Medicaid, while also advocating for protections for reproductive healthcare.

- Climate Change and the Environment: The platform prioritizes action on climate change, with a goal of achieving net-zero emissions by 2050. Democrats propose investing in renewable energy, green infrastructure, and environmental justice initiatives for communities disproportionately affected by pollution.

- LGBTQ+ Rights: The Democratic Party advocates for full legal equality for LGBTQ+ individuals. They support the Equality Act, which would make sexual orientation and gender identity protected classes in federal nondiscrimination law, ensuring broader protections for

LGBTQ+ people.

•	Economic Equality: Democrats focus on reducing income inequality, increasing taxes on the wealthy, and raising the federal minimum wage. They aim to create an economy that benefits all Americans by ensuring access to affordable healthcare, education, and childcare.

•	Voting Rights and Democracy: In light of recent voting restrictions in some states, Democrats seek to protect and expand voting rights. They advocate for reforms such as automatic voter registration, protection against voter suppression, and ensuring that elections are fair and accessible.

•	Foreign Policy: On the global stage, Democrats prioritize multilateralism, climate diplomacy, and human rights. They focus on strengthening alliances such as NATO, promoting democracy, and countering authoritarian regimes.

Republican Party - Key Views for 2024

The Republican Party's 2024 platform reflects its commitment to conservative values, with an emphasis on limiting government intervention, protecting religious freedoms, and upholding traditional family structures. Key issues include:

•	Marriage and Family: While previous platforms emphasized traditional marriage between a man and a woman, the 2024 platform takes a broader view of family support without explicitly defining marriage. Republicans focus on supporting working families and promoting the sanctity of life and marriage.

•	Abortion: Republicans are largely opposed to abortion, with many advocating for restrictions or outright bans. However, Donald Trump has stated that he does not support a national abortion ban, and this remains a divisive issue within the party. The platform emphasizes pro-life values and seeks to protect unborn children.

•	Gender and Sexuality: Republicans strongly oppose what they describe as "gender ideology." They advocate for policies that restrict transgender participation in women's sports, limit taxpayer funding for gender-affirming surgeries, and resist the Biden administration's changes to Title IX that accommodate transgender students.

•	Economy: The Republican platform focuses on free-market policies, reducing taxes, deregulation, and promoting economic growth. They argue for reducing government spending and cutting taxes to stimulate job creation and business investment.

•	Gun Rights: Republicans strongly support the Second Amendment and oppose efforts to impose stricter gun regulations. They believe in the right to bear arms as fundamental to American freedom and oppose any federal overreach that restricts gun ownership.

•	Immigration: The party continues to advocate for stronger border security and stricter immigration laws. Many Republicans support building a border wall and increasing immigration enforcement. There is also opposition to amnesty programs for undocumented immigrants.

•	Foreign Policy: Republicans emphasize national security and a strong military. The platform includes taking a hard stance on China, advocating for energy independence, and focusing on counter terrorism efforts globally.

Both candidates represent the core ideologies of their respective parties, offering voters a choice between progressive expansion of social rights and government intervention (Harris) versus conservative, nationalist policies focused on deregulation, traditional values, and limited government (Trump).

These two figures are deeply polarizing, with Biden offering continuity in progressive governance, while Trump promises a return to the disruptive, populist style that characterized his first term in office. Voters in 2024 will have to weigh these contrasting visions for the future of the United States.

CHAPTER 5.

*Presidential Elections:
Understanding the
Electoral College*

The United States presidential election process is unique and complex, largely due to the involvement of an institution known as the Electoral College. This system, established more than 200 years ago, remains a cornerstone of American democracy, despite ongoing debates over its relevance and fairness in the modern age. While many countries use direct voting to elect their leaders, the U.S. takes a different approach by using the Electoral College to formally elect the president and vice president. This essay explores the historical development, structure, and functioning of the Electoral College, including the controversies surrounding it, and evaluates its impact on U.S. presidential elections.

1. Historical Development of the Electoral College

A. Origins of the Electoral College

The Electoral College was born out of the Constitutional Convention of 1787. The founders faced a dilemma when creating the process for electing the president. They debated multiple options:

- Direct popular election: One group favored allowing the people to vote directly for the president. However, this proposal raised concerns, as many delegates feared that voters would be unfamiliar with national candidates, especially in an era with limited communication and transportation.
- Congressional selection: Another group suggested that Congress should elect the president, but this was seen as potentially making the executive too dependent on the legislative branch, undermining the balance of power.

Ultimately, the Electoral College was a compromise designed to balance the influence of small and large states, while also ensuring a degree of separation between the presidency and Congress.

B. Early Evolution and Adjustments

The framers initially envisioned that electors would exercise independent judgment when casting their votes for president. However, this notion of electors as independent actors quickly disappeared, as political parties began to nominate candidates, and electors became party loyalists pledged to vote for their party's candidates.

The first significant amendment to the Electoral College came in 1804 with the 12th Amendment, which was prompted by the election of 1800. That election exposed a flaw in the system, as Thomas Jefferson and his running mate, Aaron Burr, ended up with the same number of electoral votes, causing confusion and leading to a contingent election in the House of Representatives. The 12th Amendment ensured that electors cast separate ballots for president and vice president to prevent such ties from happening again.

2. Structure and Functioning of the Electoral College

A. Composition and Allocation of Electoral Votes

The Electoral College is composed of 538 electors. Each state is allotted a number of electors equal to the total number of its representatives in the House of Representatives plus its two senators. The District of Columbia is also granted three electors under the 23rd Amendment, although it has no voting representation in Congress.

The apportionment of electors is based on state population, which is recalculated every ten years after the U.S. Census. This gives larger states like California (55 electors), Texas (38 electors), and Florida (30 electors) more influence in the presidential election, while small states like Vermont and Wyoming still retain a minimum of three electoral votes.

B. The Voting Process

Presidential elections occur every four years on the first Tuesday in November. When voters cast their ballots, they are technically voting for a slate of electors who have pledged to support their preferred candidate. In most states, the candidate who wins the popular vote in that state takes all of its electoral votes—a system known as winner-takes-all. However, two states, Maine and Nebraska, use a district system that awards electoral votes based on both the statewide popular vote and the popular vote in each congressional district.

After the general election, the electors meet in their respective states in December to cast their official ballots for president and vice president. These votes are then sent to Congress, where they are counted in early January. To win the presidency, a candidate must receive at least 270 electoral votes, a simple majority of the 538 available.

C. Contingency Elections

If no candidate reaches the 270-vote threshold, the election is decided by a contingent election in the House of Representatives. In this scenario, each state delegation casts one vote, and a majority of states (26) is required to win. The Senate would select the vice president in a separate vote. This process has only been invoked twice, in the elections of 1800 and 1824.

3. The Impact of the Electoral College on Modern Elections

A. Emphasis on Swing States

One of the most noticeable effects of the Electoral College is the focus it places on swing states, also known as battleground states. These are states where the outcome of the election is uncertain, and both candidates have a realistic chance of winning. Swing states such as Florida, Pennsylvania, Michigan, and Wisconsin often determine the overall result of the election, as their electoral votes can swing the balance of power.

This focus on swing states means that candidates

tend to concentrate their campaigns in these regions, often neglecting states where the outcome is more predictable. For example, a Democratic candidate is unlikely to spend much time campaigning in California, which reliably votes Democratic, or in a deeply Republican state like Texas.

B. Discrepancies Between the Popular Vote and Electoral Vote

The Electoral College can result in a situation where a candidate wins the presidency without winning the popular vote. This has occurred five times in U.S. history, most notably in the 2000 and 2016 elections. In 2000, George W. Bush won the Electoral College while losing the popular vote to Al Gore. Similarly, in 2016, Donald Trump won the presidency despite receiving nearly 3 million fewer votes than Hillary Clinton.

These outcomes have fueled criticism of the Electoral College as an undemocratic system, as it allows a candidate to win the presidency even if a majority of voters prefer the opposing candidate.

C. The Winner-Takes-All System

The winner-takes-all method used by most states exacerbates the disparity between the popular vote and the electoral vote. A candidate can win a state by a narrow margin but receive all of its electoral votes, effectively nullifying the votes for the losing candidate. This system contributes to the overemphasis on swing states and the under representation of minority party voters in solidly "red" or "blue" states.

4. Criticisms of the Electoral College

The Electoral College has long been a subject of debate, with critics arguing that it is an outdated and undemocratic system, while supporters claim it serves important constitutional purposes.

A. Disproportionate Representation

One of the most common criticisms is that the Electoral College gives disproportionate representation to smaller states. Because every state receives at least three electoral votes regardless of its population, the votes of individuals in small states carry more weight than those in larger states. For example, a vote in Wyoming has significantly more electoral power than a vote in California, where the population is much larger.

B. The Role of Swing States

As mentioned earlier, the swing state phenomenon has skewed the focus of presidential campaigns. Candidates concentrate their resources and policy proposals on a handful of battleground states, while voters in other parts of the country are often ignored. This dynamic leads to uneven representation and marginalizes voters in states where the outcome is a foregone conclusion.

C. Popular Vote Discrepancies

The possibility of a candidate winning the presidency while losing the popular vote is seen by many as fundamentally unfair. Critics argue that the Electoral College distorts the democratic process by allowing the will of the majority to be overridden by the distribution of electoral votes. In response, some reformers advocate for abolishing the Electoral College in favor of a national popular vote, where the candidate with the most votes nationwide would always win.

5. Proposals for Reform

Over the years, several proposals have been made to reform or eliminate the Electoral College, though none have yet succeeded.

A. Abolition of the Electoral College

The most drastic proposal is to abolish the Electoral College entirely in favor of a national popular vote, where the candidate with the most votes nationwide would always win. While this would ensure that every vote counts equally, abolishing the system would require a constitutional amendment, a politically challenging task that requires the approval of two-thirds of Congress and three-fourths of state legislatures.

B. National Popular Vote Interstate Compact

The National Popular Vote Interstate Compact (NPVIC) is one of the most prominent efforts to reform the Electoral College without the need for a constitutional amendment. Under the NPVIC, states pledge to award their electoral votes to the candidate who wins the national popular vote, regardless of the outcome in their own state. The compact would only take effect once enough states have joined to account for at least 270 electoral votes—the number needed to win the presidency.

As of 2021, the NPVIC has been adopted by 15 states and the District of Columbia, representing a total of 196 electoral votes. However, the compact still falls short of the 270-vote threshold, and it remains unclear whether it would withstand legal challenges if it were ever implemented.

C. Proportional Allocation of Electoral Votes

Another reform proposal is to adopt a proportional allocation system for electoral votes. Under this system, each state's electoral votes would be distributed based on the percentage of the popular vote each candidate receives, rather than awarding all votes to the winner of the state. This would better reflect the will of the voters in each state and reduce the impact of swing states.

Proponents argue that proportional allocation would make elections fairer and more competitive, while opponents claim it could lead to fragmented results and increase the likelihood of no candidate receiving a majority of electoral votes, thereby triggering a contingent election in the House of Representatives.

Conclusion

The Electoral College remains a deeply ingrained institution in the U.S. political system, shaping how presidential elections are conducted and influencing the strategies of candidates. The Electoral College is a vital yet controversial institution in the U.S. political system, established to elect the president through an indirect method. Rooted in a desire to balance the power between populous and less populous states, and to ensure a degree of separation between the presidency and Congress, it has operated for over two centuries, but not without significant debate.

CHAPTER 6.

The Congressional Elections: An Overview and Analysis

Congressional elections in the United States play a crucial role in determining the legislative direction of the nation. Every two years, American citizens have the opportunity to vote for members of Congress, the legislative branch of the federal government, which is composed of two chambers: the House of Representatives and the Senate. These elections, while often overshadowed by presidential elections, are equally important as they shape the country's laws, influence policies, and impact the balance of power between the executive and legislative branches.

Structure of Congress

Before diving into the details of congressional elections, it's important to understand the structure of Congress. The U.S. Congress is a bicameral legislature, meaning it has two chambers: the House of Representatives and the Senate.

• The House of Representatives consists of 435 members who serve two-year terms. Representation in the House is based on the population of each state, with more populous states having more representatives. Every two years, all 435 seats in the House are up for election.

• The Senate consists of 100 members, with each state having two senators, regardless of its population. Senators serve six-year terms, and every two years, approximately one-third of the Senate is up for re-election.

Types of Congressional Elections

Congressional elections can be divided into two types:

1. General Elections: Held every two years on the first Tuesday after the first Monday in November, these elections determine who will fill the seats in the House of Representatives and one-third of the Senate. General elections occur in even-numbered years and coincide with presidential elections every four years.

2. Midterm Elections: These are general elections that take place halfway through a president's four-year term. During midterms, all House seats and about one-third of Senate seats are contested, but there is no presidential election. Midterm elections often serve as a referendum on the sitting president's performance, with the president's party historically losing seats.

Importance of Congressional Elections

Congressional elections are fundamental to the functioning of American democracy. The elected members of Congress are responsible for making federal laws, shaping domestic and foreign policies, and providing checks and balances on the executive branch. These elections offer voters the chance to have a direct say in the composition of the legislative body that will influence the country's direction on critical issues, such as healthcare, immigration, taxation, and national security.

Moreover, congressional elections play a key role in determining the balance of power between the two major political parties—the Democrats and the Republicans. If one party gains a majority in either the House or the Senate, it can significantly influence the legislative agenda, appoint committee chairs, and impact the overall direction of policy making.

The Election Process

1. The House of Representatives

Members of the House are elected from 435 congressional districts, each of which is designed to have roughly equal populations, although district lines are redrawn every ten years following the national census (a process called redistricting). States may gain or lose districts depending on population shifts, but the total number of House members remains fixed.

- Primary Elections: Before the general election, primary elections are held, typically in the spring or summer, where each party selects its candidate. These primaries can be closed (only party members can vote) or open (any registered voter can participate), depending on the state's laws.

- General Elections: In November, the general election takes place. The candidate with the most votes in each district wins, using a first-past-the-post system, meaning that they do not need to win a majority, just more votes than their opponents.

2. The Senate

Senators serve six-year terms, with elections staggered so that only about one-third of the Senate is up for election every two years. Unlike House elections, senators are elected statewide, meaning they represent their entire state rather than individual districts.

- Primary Elections: Similar to the House, primaries are held to select each party's candidate for Senate races. These primaries vary in competitiveness depending on the state and the incumbent's popularity.

- General Elections: In the general election, the candidate who wins the most votes becomes the senator for that state. As with House races, Senate races use a first-past-the-post system.

Voter Eligibility and Participation

In congressional elections, voter eligibility

follows the same rules as in other U.S. elections. Citizens must be at least 18 years old and meet their state's residency and registration requirements. However, voter turnout in congressional elections, particularly midterms, tends to be lower than in presidential elections. Historically, midterms attract about 40% of eligible voters, while presidential elections often see around 60% voter turnout.

Role of Political Parties

Political parties play a critical role in congressional elections by:

- Endorsing and Supporting Candidates: Parties support their candidates through funding, strategic advice, and volunteer mobilization. Party organizations like the Democratic Congressional Campaign Committee (DCCC) and the National Republican Congressional Committee (NRCC) are instrumental in funding campaigns and crafting electoral strategies.

- Shaping the Agenda: Parties craft platforms and messaging that candidates align with, helping to create a national narrative for the election. For example, Democrats may focus on healthcare, climate change, and social justice, while Republicans might emphasize tax cuts, deregulation, and immigration control.

- Mobilizing Voters: Parties conduct extensive voter outreach, utilizing both traditional means like door-to-door canvassing and modern methods such as digital and social media campaigning.

Gerrymandering and Its Impact

One of the most controversial aspects of congressional elections, particularly in the House, is gerrymandering—the practice of redrawing district boundaries to favor one political party. Gerrymandering can significantly affect election outcomes by concentrating or dispersing voters of a particular party across districts, making some districts safe for one party and others highly competitive.

There are two main types of gerrymandering:

- Partisan Gerrymandering: This is done to benefit a particular political party. For example, a state controlled by Republicans might draw district lines to pack Democratic voters into a few districts while ensuring that Republicans have a slight majority in several others, giving them more overall seats.

- Racial Gerrymandering: This refers to drawing districts in a way that dilutes the voting power of racial minority groups, often violating the Voting Rights Act of 1965. Courts have intervened in many instances of racial gerrymandering, but it remains a contentious issue.

Gerrymandering has profound implications for congressional elections, often leading to a lack of competitiveness in many districts, which can discourage voter turnout and reinforce political polarization.

Incumbency Advantage

One of the notable features of congressional elections is the incumbency advantage.

Incumbents—those already holding office—have several advantages over challengers, including:

- Name Recognition: Voters are more likely to recognize the name of the incumbent, which can influence their vote.

- Fundraising Ability: Incumbents often have established networks of donors and can raise more money for their campaigns than challengers.

- Constituent Services: Incumbents have the ability to engage in constituency work, helping local citizens with federal services, which can boost their popularity.

- Media Access: Incumbents are often more visible in the media, giving them more opportunities to reach voters.

Because of these advantages, incumbents are re-elected at very high rates. In recent years, over 90% of House incumbents and around 80-90% of Senate incumbents have won re-election.

Midterm Elections and Presidential Coattails

Midterm elections are often seen as a referendum on the sitting president and his party. Historically, the party that controls the White House tends to lose seats in Congress during midterms. This trend is known as the midterm penalty and has affected presidents from both parties.

The reasons for this pattern include:

- Voter Discontent: Midterms often reflect

dissatisfaction with the sitting president's policies or performance. Voters may use midterms to express their frustration, especially if the president's approval ratings are low.

• Lower Turnout: Midterm elections typically have lower voter turnout compared to presidential elections. The voters who do turn out are often more politically motivated and may be driven by opposition to the president's party.

On the other hand, in presidential election years, the president's popularity can help congressional candidates from their party, a phenomenon known as presidential coattails. Candidates from the same party as a popular presidential candidate may receive a boost simply by association, helping them win tight races.

Congressional Committees and Leadership

After congressional elections, one of the most significant outcomes is the establishment of congressional leadership and the composition of committees. Leadership in both the House and Senate is determined by the majority party, with the Speaker of the House being one of the most powerful positions in the government.

Committees play a crucial role in the legislative process, as they are responsible for drafting, reviewing, and amending bills before they reach the full chamber for a vote. The majority party in each chamber controls the chairmanship of all committees, giving them substantial influence over the legislative agenda.

Understanding The Structure Of Congress

Congress is a bicameral legislature, divided into two chambers: the House of Representatives and the Senate.

1. The House of Representatives

The House consists of 435 members, with each state's representation based on its population size. This ensures that more populous states like California and Texas have more representatives, while smaller states like Vermont and Wyoming have only one representative. Every member of the House is elected for a two-year term, meaning all seats are up for election every two years.

2. The Senate

The Senate, on the other hand, consists of 100 members, with each state having two senators, regardless of population size. Senators serve six-year terms, and their elections are staggered so that only one-third of the Senate is up for election every two years. This staggered schedule ensures stability and continuity within the Senate, even as new representatives are elected to the House.

Together, the House and Senate form Congress,

which plays a critical role in drafting, debating, and passing federal laws. Additionally, Congress provides oversight of the executive branch and ensures that government policies reflect the will of the people.

The Election Process

1. House of Representatives Elections

House elections take place every two years, and each state is divided into congressional districts that are drawn based on population. These districts are redrawn every 10 years after the U.S. Census in a process known as redistricting. Redistricting can lead to gerrymandering, where district boundaries are manipulated to favor one political party, often leading to less competitive elections.

Each district elects one representative, and the candidate who receives the most votes wins the election. This is known as the first-past-the-post system, meaning a candidate does not need to win a majority but simply a plurality of votes to be elected.

2. Senate Elections

Senators are elected on a statewide basis, as each state is a single Senate district. Unlike House elections, Senate elections happen every six years, with one-third of the Senate elected during each two-year election cycle. The same first-past-the-post system applies in Senate elections, where the candidate with the most votes wins.

3. Primary and General Elections

Before the general election in November, candidates from each party typically compete in primary elections held earlier in the year. These primaries decide which candidates will represent their party in the general election. Some states have closed primaries, where only registered party members can vote, while others have open primaries, where any registered voter can participate, regardless of party affiliation.

In general elections, candidates from each party, as well as any independent or third-party candidates, compete for the seat. General elections take place on the first Tuesday after the first Monday in November of even-numbered years.

Voter Participation in Congressional Elections

Voter turnout in congressional elections varies widely. In presidential election years, turnout is typically higher as the presidential race draws more voters to the polls. However, during midterm elections, which take place halfway through a president's four-year term, turnout tends to be lower. This is a significant factor because midterms often serve as a referendum on the president's performance, and historically, the president's party tends to lose seats in both the House and Senate during midterms.

Several factors influence voter turnout in congressional elections, including:

- Voter Enthusiasm: When important national issues are at stake, such as healthcare reform or immigration policy, voter enthusiasm tends to increase, leading to higher turnout.

- Voter Suppression: In some states, voter ID laws, reduced early voting periods, and restrictive voter registration practices may reduce turnout, particularly among minority and low-income voters.

- Voting Accessibility: Conversely, states that make voting more accessible through measures like automatic voter registration, mail-in voting, and early voting options often see higher turnout rates.

The Role of Political Parties

Political parties, particularly the Democratic Party and the Republican Party, play an essential role in congressional elections. The two-party system dominates American politics, with Democrats and Republicans typically controlling the majority of seats in Congress. Political parties:

- Select Candidates: Through the primary election process, parties select candidates to represent their platforms and values in the general election.

- Fund Campaigns: Parties provide

significant financial support to their candidates, funding campaign advertisements, rallies, and other outreach efforts.

•	Shape Policy Agendas: Each party has a distinct platform that outlines its policy goals. For example, in recent years, Democrats have emphasized expanding healthcare access, addressing climate change, and ensuring social justice, while Republicans have focused on cutting taxes, reducing government regulation, and strengthening border security.

Party Control and Legislative Power

When one party controls the majority of seats in either the House or Senate, they can significantly influence the legislative process. The majority party appoints the leadership of the chamber and controls the agenda by deciding which bills come to the floor for debate and votes. In the House, the Speaker of the House is the most powerful position, while in the Senate, the Senate Majority Leader holds significant sway.

When Congress is divided—with one party controlling the House and the other controlling the Senate—it can lead to legislative gridlock, where little meaningful legislation is passed due to partisan disagreements.

Gerrymandering and Its Impact on Congressional Elections

One of the most controversial aspects of congressional elections is gerrymandering.

Gerrymandering occurs when the party in control of a state's legislature redraws congressional district boundaries to benefit their party. This often leads to safe seats for incumbents and fewer competitive elections, as district boundaries are drawn to dilute the opposition party's voter base.

Gerrymandering has profound implications for congressional elections because it can skew representation in the House, making it difficult for the minority party to win seats in highly gerrymandered states. Courts have ruled against extreme forms of racial gerrymandering, but partisan gerrymandering remains a persistent issue.

Key Issues in Congressional Elections

Congressional elections often revolve around critical national issues that resonate with voters. The importance of these issues can vary from election to election, depending on the political climate, economic conditions, and public opinion. Some key issues in recent congressional elections include:

1. Healthcare

Healthcare remains a dominant issue in congressional elections, particularly following the passage of the Affordable Care Act (ACA) in 2010. Democrats have generally supported expanding healthcare access, while Republicans have sought to repeal or modify the ACA, advocating for more market-driven solutions.

2. The Economy

Economic issues, such as unemployment, income inequality, and taxation, are always central to congressional campaigns. Republicans tend to advocate for tax cuts, deregulation, and pro-business policies, while Democrats focus on increasing the minimum wage, addressing wage inequality, and expanding government programs for the poor and middle class.

3. Immigration

Immigration policy has been highly divisive, especially during the Trump administration, when immigration enforcement and border security became focal points of political debate. Republicans often emphasize strict border control and immigration enforcement, while Democrats tend to support comprehensive immigration reform, including pathways to citizenship for undocumented immigrants.

4. Climate Change

In recent years, climate change has become a critical issue, particularly among younger voters and progressives. Democrats advocate for bold climate action, such as transitioning to renewable energy sources and reducing carbon emissions. Republicans, however, are more likely to prioritize economic concerns over environmental regulation, arguing that climate policies could harm industries like oil and gas.

5. Gun Control

The debate over gun control has intensified following a series of mass shootings in the U.S. Democrats generally support stronger gun control measures, such as background checks and restrictions on assault weapons, while Republicans typically defend the right to bear arms, emphasizing the importance of the Second Amendment.

6. Abortion and Reproductive Rights

Abortion has been a central issue following the Supreme Court's decision to overturn *Roe v. Wade*. Democrats advocate for protecting and expanding access to reproductive healthcare, while Republicans have supported state-level restrictions on abortion rights.

Conclusion: The Impact of Congressional Elections

Congressional elections are a vital aspect of

American democracy, directly influencing the nation's legislative process and balance of power. They offer citizens the opportunity to elect representatives who reflect their views and priorities on key issues such as healthcare, the economy, immigration, and more. Political parties play a central role in shaping these elections, from selecting candidates to defining policy agendas.

Despite the lower voter turnout in midterm elections, the outcomes of congressional races have profound implications for the country's political landscape. They determine whether the president's party can pass its legislative agenda or face opposition from a divided or hostile Congress. Ultimately, congressional elections ensure that the U.S. government remains accountable to the people, providing an essential check on executive power and shaping the nation's future.

CHAPTER 7.

*Understanding the Voting
Process in the United States*

Voting in the United States is the foundation of its democratic system, providing citizens with the ability to influence their government by selecting representatives at local, state, and national levels. The U.S. voting process is designed to ensure that citizens can freely express their political preferences, but it involves several steps and regulations that vary across states and territories. This essay provides an in-depth explanation of the U.S. voting process, covering voter registration, types of elections, voting methods, and the various ways in which citizens can cast their ballots.

Voter Registration: The First Step In Voting

One of the fundamental steps in the U.S.

voting process is voter registration. Unlike in some countries where citizens are automatically registered to vote, the U.S. requires eligible citizens to actively register. To be eligible to vote, individuals must meet specific criteria:

- Citizenship: Only U.S. citizens can vote in federal, state, and most local elections.
- Age: Voters must be at least 18 years old on or before election day.
- Residency: Voters must be residents of the state and sometimes the district where they plan to vote.
- Criminal Record: Some states restrict voting rights for individuals convicted of felonies, though recent reforms in several states have restored voting rights to some individuals who have completed their sentences.

Voter registration typically involves filling out a form either online, by mail, or in person at various locations such as the Department of Motor Vehicles (DMV), public assistance offices, or local election offices. Many states have introduced automatic voter registration (AVR), where eligible citizens are automatically registered to vote when they interact with government agencies unless they choose to opt out. Additionally, some states offer same-day registration, allowing voters to register and vote on the same day.

The deadline for registering to vote varies by state, with most requiring voters to register at least 30 days before an election, although some states offer registration up to election day. Once registered, voters remain on the voter rolls unless they move, pass away, or are removed due to inactivity.

Types of Elections

In the United States, elections are held for various offices and purposes, ranging from local to federal levels. The key types of elections include:

1. Primary Elections: Primaries determine which candidates will represent their political parties in the general election. There are two main types of primaries:

- Open Primaries: In open primaries, any registered voter, regardless of party affiliation, can vote in any party's primary.
- Closed Primaries: In closed primaries, only voters who are registered members of a party can vote in that party's primary.

2. General Elections: General elections occur every two years in November and are held to elect members of Congress, state legislators, governors, and other officials. Every four years, the general election includes the presidential race.

3. Midterm Elections: Midterms are general elections that occur halfway through a president's term (every two years). During midterms, voters elect all members of the House of Representatives and one-third of the Senate.

4. Special Elections: These elections are held to fill vacant positions due to resignations, deaths, or other circumstances.

5.   Ballot Initiatives and Referenda: In some states, voters can also vote directly on policy proposals, constitutional amendments, or other measures through ballot initiatives or referenda.

Voting Methods

Once registered, voters have several methods for casting their ballots. These options are designed to accommodate various preferences and circumstances, allowing voters to participate even if they cannot be present at a polling location on election day.

1. In-Person Voting

Traditionally, the most common method of voting is by casting a ballot in person at a designated polling place. Polling places are often set up in public buildings such as schools, community centers, or libraries. To vote in person, individuals go to their assigned polling place, verify their identity (in some states, photo identification is required), and then cast their ballot, either on paper or using an electronic voting machine.

Polling places are open from early morning until the evening, typically from 7:00 a.m. to 8:00 p.m., though hours vary by state. Early voting is another option for in-person voting, which allows voters to cast their ballots before election day. Early voting can take place at special polling centers or government offices, and it usually begins a few weeks before election day.

2. Absentee and Mail-In Voting

Absentee voting allows voters who cannot be present on election day to vote by mail. Historically, absentee voting was used by military personnel, people traveling, or those with illnesses or disabilities. However, in recent years, especially during the COVID-19 pandemic, mail-in voting has become more widely available.

In many states, voters can request a mail-in ballot without providing a reason (known as no-excuse absentee voting), while other states require voters to meet specific criteria. Some states, such as Colorado, Oregon, and Washington, conduct their elections entirely by mail, automatically sending ballots to all registered voters.

Mail-in ballots must be completed and returned by mail or dropped off at designated locations, often including secure drop boxes. Each ballot must be signed by the voter, and many states require signature verification to ensure the integrity of the process. Depending on the state, mail-in ballots must either be received by election day or postmarked by election day and received shortly thereafter.

3. Provisional Ballots

If there is an issue with a voter's eligibility on election day—such as their name not appearing on the voter rolls or a lack of proper identification—they may be allowed to cast a provisional ballot. Provisional ballots are set aside and only counted once the voter's eligibility is confirmed.

For example, if a voter forgets to bring the required identification to the polling place, they may cast a provisional ballot and later provide identification to the election office to have their vote counted.

Ensuring Election Security and Integrity

Given the importance of fair elections, the U.S. takes multiple measures to ensure the integrity of the voting process. These safeguards include:

- Voter ID Laws: Some states require voters to present identification at the polling place. The types of acceptable ID vary, but common forms include driver's licenses, state-issued IDs, passports, and military IDs. While proponents argue that ID laws prevent voter fraud, opponents claim that they disproportionately affect low-income and minority voters who may not have easy access to ID.

- Election Monitoring: Polling places are often monitored by bipartisan election officials and observers to ensure that voting is conducted fairly and that no improper activity occurs. Some states also allow independent observers from political parties or nongovernmental organizations to oversee the voting process.

•   Post-Election Audits: After the election, many states conduct audits to verify the accuracy of the vote count. This may involve recounting ballots in a sample of precincts or checking the performance of voting machines.

•   Provisional Ballot Verification: Provisional ballots are verified to ensure that only eligible voters have their votes counted. This includes confirming that the voter is registered and eligible to vote in the given election.

•   Cybersecurity Measures: With the increasing reliance on electronic systems, the U.S. government has invested in cybersecurity measures to protect election infrastructure from hacking and other cyber threats. Agencies like the Department of Homeland Security work closely with state and local governments to monitor and prevent cyberattacks.

Voter Participation and Challenges

While voting is the cornerstone of U.S. democracy, not all eligible citizens choose to participate in elections. Voter turnout varies widely depending on the type of election, with presidential elections typically drawing more voters than midterms or local elections. For instance, in the 2020 presidential election, turnout reached a historic high of over 66%, but turnout in midterm elections generally hovers around 40%.

Several factors influence voter participation:

•   Access and Convenience: Voter turnout tends to be higher in states that make voting more convenient, such as offering early voting, no-excuse absentee voting, or automatic voter registration.

• Voter Suppression: Voter suppression tactics, such as strict voter ID laws, purges of voter rolls, or reduced polling locations, can discourage or prevent eligible citizens from voting. These tactics often disproportionately affect minority groups, the elderly, and low-income individuals.

• Voter Engagement: The perceived importance of an election can also influence turnout. In elections where key issues like healthcare, the economy, or civil rights are at stake, voters may feel more compelled to participate.

Conclusion

The U.S. voting process is a complex system designed to ensure that citizens can actively participate in their democracy. While it involves several steps—from registration to casting a ballot—it offers various options to accommodate voters' needs, including in-person, absentee, and early voting. Safeguards are in place to ensure election integrity, though challenges such as voter suppression and disparities in access continue to affect voter participation. Despite these challenges, voting remains the most fundamental way for U.S. citizens to influence their government and shape the policies that impact their daily lives.

CHAPTER 8.

How Votes Are Counted: A Comprehensive Overview

Vote counting is one of the most critical aspects of any election process, determining the outcome of races for local, state, and federal offices. In the United States, the counting of votes involves multiple layers of security, transparency, and verification to ensure that every valid vote is counted accurately. This essay provides a detailed explanation of how votes are counted in U.S. elections, covering the processes for different voting methods, safeguards to ensure accuracy, and the roles of election officials in maintaining the integrity of the election results.

Types of Voting Methods and Their Counting Process

The vote counting process varies based on the type of ballot cast—whether it is an in-person paper ballot, a machine-readable ballot, or a mail-in ballot. The method used can influence how quickly and accurately votes are tabulated.

1. Paper Ballots

Paper ballots are the most traditional form of voting and remain in use in many parts of the United States. Voters mark their choices on paper, and the ballots are either counted manually or fed into an optical scanner that reads and tallies the votes.

- Manual Counting: In smaller elections or precincts, election workers may count paper ballots by hand. Each ballot is examined for marks that clearly indicate the voter's choice. Election workers, usually working in bipartisan teams, verify that the ballot is valid and then add it to the vote total.

- Machine Counting: In many places, paper ballots are scanned by optical scanners. These machines read the marks on each ballot and immediately tally the votes, which are then stored in a digital database. The scanners can process thousands of ballots per hour, making this a highly efficient method of counting. However, the paper ballots remain on hand for verification or recounts if needed.

Optical scanners are commonly used for in-person voting, but they can also be used for counting mail-in ballots that are designed in a similar format. This combination of physical and digital record-keeping ensures that there is always a paper trail for auditing purposes.

2. Electronic Voting Machines

In some areas, voters use direct-recording electronic (DRE) voting machines, which allow them to make their selections directly on a touchscreen or push-button device. These machines store the votes digitally, and in some cases, they print a paper receipt that allows voters to verify their choices before finalizing the vote.

• Instant Tallying: DRE machines tally votes as they are cast, meaning results from these machines can be quickly totaled at the end of the voting day. The machines automatically store vote data in a secure electronic format, which is then transmitted to a central counting facility.

• Audit and Verification: Many jurisdictions using DRE machines also require that a voter-verified paper audit trail (VVPAT) be printed after the vote is cast. This paper trail allows for a manual recount if the electronic results are questioned, adding another layer of security to the vote count.

3. Mail-In and Absentee Ballots

Mail-in ballots, also referred to as absentee ballots, have become increasingly popular in recent elections, especially following the COVID-19 pandemic. The counting process for mail-in ballots is slightly more complex due to the need to verify voter information before the ballot is counted.

• Verification Process: Before counting, each

mail-in ballot must be verified. Election officials check the voter's signature on the ballot envelope against the signature on file. In some cases, the voter may need to include additional identifying information, such as a driver's license number or the last four digits of their Social Security number.

•   Counting the Ballots: Once verified, mail-in ballots are typically fed into optical scanners to be counted. Some jurisdictions begin processing mail-in ballots before election day, though most do not start tabulating the results until the polls have closed.

•   Handling Discrepancies: If a ballot contains an error, such as an unclear mark or an incomplete signature, election officials may set it aside as a "provisional" or "challenged" ballot. These ballots are usually reviewed by a bipartisan team of election workers who determine whether the vote should be counted.

Safeguards to Ensure Accuracy and Integrity

The U.S. election system incorporates numerous safeguards to ensure that the vote counting process is accurate, secure, and transparent. These safeguards include checks on election workers, security for ballots, and audits of the results.

1. Bipartisan Oversight

One of the most important safeguards in the vote counting process is the involvement of bipartisan teams of election workers. By requiring that representatives from both major political parties participate in vote counting, the system reduces the potential for partisan bias or fraud. Observers from political parties, candidates, and independent organizations are often allowed to monitor the counting process to ensure transparency.

2. Chain of Custody

The chain of custody refers to the process of ensuring that ballots are securely handled from the moment they are cast until the results are certified. Each step in the process is documented, and only authorized personnel are allowed to handle ballots. This prevents tampering or misplacement of ballots during the counting process.

In some states, election officials transport ballots in sealed containers, accompanied by signed documentation that tracks their movement. Chain of custody procedures are especially important for mail-in ballots, which may be handled by multiple entities, including the postal service, before reaching election officials.

3. Provisional Ballots

Provisional ballots are used when there is a question about a voter's eligibility, such as when a voter's name does not appear on the voter rolls or when the voter lacks proper identification.

Provisional ballots are kept separate from other ballots until election officials can verify the voter's eligibility.

Each provisional ballot is reviewed individually. If the voter is found to be eligible, the ballot is counted. If not, the ballot is discarded. This process ensures that no ineligible votes are included in the final tally while also protecting the rights of voters who may have encountered issues at the polling place.

4. Recounts and Audits

Recounts are often triggered when the margin of victory is extremely narrow or when a candidate requests one. Recounts can be conducted manually or by machine, depending on state laws. In some cases, recounts are automatic when the difference in vote totals between candidates is within a certain percentage—typically 0.5% or less.

In addition to recounts, many states conduct post-election audits to ensure the accuracy of the vote count. Audits typically involve reviewing a random sample of ballots and comparing them to the reported results. These audits help to detect any errors or irregularities in the vote count, ensuring public confidence in the results.

How Results Are Reported

The process of reporting election results begins as soon as polls close on election day. Election officials at each polling location or counting center begin transmitting preliminary vote totals to a central location. These results are often reported in stages, with initial tallies consisting of in-person votes followed by absentee or mail-in ballots.

1. Early and Election Day Voting Results

• Election Day Voting: Polling places close at a designated time, and election officials immediately begin counting the in-person votes. In many cases, local results are available within hours of the polls closing, especially for smaller precincts or those using electronic voting machines.

• Early Voting: Some jurisdictions report early voting results as soon as the polls close. Early voting totals are often included in the first wave of reported results, providing an initial look at the race before all ballots are counted.

2. Mail-In and Absentee Ballot Results

• Time Lag: Absentee and mail-in ballots take longer to count, especially in states where a large percentage of the electorate votes by mail. This delay is due to the time required for verifying signatures and processing each ballot. In some states, ballots postmarked by election day are accepted even if they arrive several days later, meaning the final results may not be available for several days or even weeks.

• Late Ballots: States with high rates of mail-in voting typically see more delays in finalizing results, as mail-in ballots often arrive after election day but before the final counting deadline. Election officials must be meticulous in counting these votes, which can sometimes shift the outcome of close races.

The Certification of Election Results

After all ballots have been counted and any recounts or challenges resolved, the election results are certified by election officials. Certification is the formal process of confirming that the vote totals are accurate and that the election was conducted in accordance with state and federal laws.

- Local Certification: Each county or jurisdiction certifies its results first, sending them to the state election authority.

- State Certification: Once all counties or localities have certified their results, the state conducts its own review and certifies the statewide results. In some states, the governor or a designated election board must sign off on the certification.

Once certified, the election results are final, and the winning candidates can officially take office.

Conclusion

The U.S. vote counting process is designed to balance speed with accuracy, ensuring that election results are reported as quickly as possible while maintaining the highest standards of integrity. From verifying mail-in ballots to conducting audits and recounts, the system includes numerous safeguards to prevent errors and protect the democratic process. While the methods of counting may vary depending on the type of ballot and the jurisdiction, the overarching goal remains the same: to ensure that every valid vote is counted and that the will of the people is reflected in the election results.

CHAPTER 9.

*Challenges and Controversies
in U.S. Elections:*

*A Comprehensive
Examination*

The U.S. electoral system, though a cornerstone of its democracy, faces several challenges and controversies that have been magnified in recent decades. While the right to vote and the principle of fair elections are foundational to the American political landscape, multiple issues ranging from voter suppression and gerrymandering to misinformation and foreign interference have raised concerns about the integrity of the electoral process. In this essay, we will explore the key challenges and controversies surrounding U.S. elections, analyze their historical development, and discuss their impact on democracy.

1. Voter Suppression

Voter suppression refers to strategies and policies that are implemented to prevent certain groups of people from voting or make it more difficult for them to do so. Historically, voter suppression has been used to disenfranchise African Americans, women, and other marginalized groups in the United States.

A. Historical Roots of Voter Suppression

The roots of voter suppression can be traced back to the Reconstruction Era (1865–1877), when African American men were granted the right to vote through the 15th Amendment. However, Southern states quickly introduced Jim Crow laws and other barriers, such as literacy tests, poll taxes, and the "grandfather clause," to prevent Black citizens from voting. Although the Voting Rights Act of 1965 outlawed many of these practices, modern-day voter suppression still exists in more subtle forms.

B. Modern Forms of Voter Suppression

Today, voter suppression tactics often take the form of strict voter ID laws, restrictions on early voting, purging voter rolls, and limiting the number of polling places in certain areas, particularly those with a high concentration of minority voters. For example, voter ID laws, which require voters to present government-issued identification at the polls, have been criticized for disproportionately affecting minorities, the elderly, and low-income individuals who may not have easy access to identification documents.

Another controversial tactic is the purging of voter rolls, where states remove inactive voters from the voter registry. While this is done to prevent fraud, it can result in legitimate voters being unable to cast their ballots. For instance, a 2018 report revealed that over 17 million voters had been purged from the rolls between 2016 and 2018.

C. Impact on Elections

Voter suppression has a profound effect on election outcomes, particularly in closely contested races. For example, in the 2018 Georgia gubernatorial race, allegations of voter suppression became a central issue, with claims that restrictive voting laws disproportionately affected African American voters, contributing to a narrow victory for the Republican candidate. The perception of voter suppression undermines trust in the democratic process and fuels political polarization.

2. Gerrymandering

Gerrymandering refers to the manipulation of electoral district boundaries to favor one political party over another. This practice distorts the principle of equal representation, often leading to skewed electoral outcomes.

A. Partisan Gerrymandering

Partisan gerrymandering occurs when the party in control of a state's legislature redraws district lines in a way that maximizes its chances of winning a disproportionate number of seats. This can be done through two main tactics:

- "Packing": Concentrating as many voters of the opposing party as possible into a single district, thereby reducing their influence in other districts.
- "Cracking": Spreading opposition voters across multiple districts so that they do not form a majority in any of them.

Both techniques result in distorted representation, where the number of seats won by a party does not accurately reflect the proportion of votes it received. A prime example of partisan gerrymandering can be seen in the state of North Carolina, where the congressional map was repeatedly redrawn to favor Republicans, even though the state's voters were closely divided between the two parties .

B. Racial Gerrymandering

Racial gerrymandering involves drawing district boundaries in a way that dilutes the voting power of racial minorities. Although the Voting Rights Act prohibits racial discrimination in redistricting, many cases of racial gerrymandering have emerged, particularly in Southern states with significant African American populations. In 2017, the Supreme Court ruled that North Carolina had unconstitutionally drawn two congressional districts based on race, reaffirming that racial gerrymandering is illegal .

C. Legal and Political Challenges

The legality of partisan gerrymandering has been a contentious issue. In 2019, the U.S. Supreme Court ruled in Rucho v. Common Cause that partisan gerrymandering claims were beyond the reach of federal courts, effectively leaving it up to state legislatures and courts to address the issue. This decision was controversial because it allows partisan gerrymandering to continue unchecked in many states.

3. Election Security and Foreign Interference

The integrity of U.S. elections has come under increased scrutiny in recent years due to concerns about cybersecurity and foreign interference.

A. The 2016 Presidential Election and Russian Interference

The most notable instance of foreign interference occurred during the 2016 U.S. presidential election, when the Russian government was found to have conducted a coordinated campaign to influence the election outcome. According to investigations by U.S. intelligence agencies, Russian actors used social media disinformation campaigns, cyberattacks on state voting systems, and the hacking of political party emails to sow discord and undermine trust in the electoral process .

B. Cybersecurity Challenges

In response to the growing threat of foreign interference, election security has become a top priority for federal, state, and local governments. Efforts to protect the election system include upgrading voting machines, increasing cybersecurity measures, and conducting post-election audits to verify results. However, the U.S. election system remains vulnerable due to its decentralized nature, with each state having its own election procedures and infrastructure.

For example, many states still use outdated electronic voting machines that lack a paper trail, making it difficult to verify the accuracy of the vote count in case of a cyberattack. While several states have moved to adopt paper-based systems or introduce risk-limiting audits, election security remains an ongoing challenge .

4. Misinformation and Disinformation

The rise of social media has made it easier for misinformation and disinformation to spread, posing a significant challenge to the integrity of elections.

A. The Role of Social Media

Platforms like Facebook, Twitter, and YouTube have been used to spread false information about candidates, voting procedures, and the election process. During the 2020 presidential election, false claims about widespread voter fraud and the security of mail-in voting proliferated online, contributing to widespread distrust in the electoral system. These claims, many of which were promoted by political figures, were not based on evidence but had a significant impact on public perception.

B. Consequences of Misinformation

Misinformation erodes trust in the democratic

process, leading voters to question the legitimacy of election outcomes. For instance, after the 2020 presidential election, the widespread belief in voter fraud—despite numerous investigations finding no evidence of systemic fraud—led to the January 6, 2021, attack on the U.S. Capitol, where supporters of the outgoing president sought to overturn the election results.

Combating misinformation is a complex challenge, as social media platforms grapple with balancing the need for free expression with the responsibility to prevent the spread of harmful falsehoods. Despite efforts by platforms to remove or label false content, misinformation continues to play a role in shaping public opinion around elections .

5. Disparities in Voter Access and Turnout

Disparities in voter access and turnout are another significant challenge in U.S. elections. Factors such as socio-economic status, race, age, and geographic location can influence a person's ability to vote and the likelihood of their vote being counted.

A. Socio-Economic and Geographic Barriers

Voter access varies significantly across the country. For instance, rural areas may have fewer polling places, making it more difficult for residents to cast their votes. Additionally, socio-economic barriers, such as lack of transportation, childcare, or inflexible work schedules, disproportionately affect low-income voters.

In some states, restrictions on early voting and absentee voting exacerbate these challenges. For example, some states require voters to provide a reason for voting absentee, while others have eliminated or reduced early voting periods. These restrictions disproportionately affect voters who may not be able to vote on election day due to work or family obligations .

B. Voter Turnout Disparities

Voter turnout in the U.S. also varies by demographic group. Historically, white, older, and wealthier voters are more likely to vote, while minority groups, young voters, and low-income individuals are underrepresented. This disparity in turnout can influence election outcomes, particularly in local and state races.

Efforts to increase voter turnout, such as automatic voter registration, expanding early voting, and mail-in voting, have been implemented in some states to address these disparities. However, the effectiveness of these measures varies, and turnout remains a key challenge in U.S. elections .

6. Electoral College and "Winner-Takes-All" System

The Electoral College system, used to elect the president, is another source of controversy in U.S. elections. The winner-takes-all system, used by most states, means that the candidate who wins the popular vote in a state receives all of that state's electoral votes.

A. Disproportionate Influence of Swing States

One of the key criticisms of the Electoral College is that it gives disproportionate influence to swing states—states where the outcome of the election is uncertain. Candidates focus their campaigns on these states, while voters in reliably Democratic or Republican states receive less attention.

B. Winner-Takes-All System

Most states use a winner-takes-all system, where the candidate who wins the popular vote in the state receives all of its electoral votes. This system can result in situations where a candidate who wins the national popular vote loses the election due to the distribution of electoral votes. For example, in the 2016 election, Hillary Clinton won the popular vote by nearly 3 million votes, but Donald Trump won the presidency by securing more electoral votes.

C. Calls for Reform

There have been numerous calls to reform or abolish the Electoral College, with some advocating for a national popular vote. Proponents of reform argue that every vote should count equally, while opponents claim that the Electoral College protects the interests of smaller states and ensures regional diversity in presidential campaigns.

6. Disparities in Voter Turnout

Disparities in voter turnout are another significant issue in U.S. elections, with racial, age, and socio-economic factors influencing who participates in the democratic process.

A. Racial and Socioeconomic Disparities

Historically, white, wealthier, and older voters have turned out in greater numbers than minorities, low-income individuals, and young voters. Structural barriers such as strict voter ID laws, lack of early voting options, and limited polling locations exacerbate these disparities.

B. Efforts to Increase Turnout

To address these disparities, some states have implemented reforms such as automatic voter registration, same-day registration, and expanded early voting options. These measures have been shown to increase voter participation, particularly among underrepresented groups. However, in states where restrictive voting laws persist, turnout disparities remain a significant challenge.

Conclusion: A Path Forward

The challenges and controversies in U.S. elections are deeply rooted and multifaceted, ranging from voter suppression and gerrymandering to election security and misinformation. Addressing these issues requires a concerted effort from lawmakers, civil society, and voters themselves to ensure that the electoral process is fair, transparent, and representative. While some progress has been made in areas such as election security and voter access, the U.S. electoral system continues to face significant hurdles that must be addressed to safeguard the future of American democracy.

CONCLUSION

Understanding the U.S. election system is critical for several reasons, as it directly influences the functioning of democracy, civic engagement, and the protection of rights. Here's why it matters:

1. Empowerment and Civic Responsibility

Understanding the U.S. election system empowers citizens to participate effectively in democracy. Voting is a key mechanism through which individuals influence government policies, leadership, and decisions that affect their lives. An informed voter can make choices based on a clear understanding of how the process works, who the candidates are, and what policies they represent. Without this knowledge, citizens may be less motivated to vote or could be misinformed about how to vote properly, leading to decreased civic participation.

2. Influence of Elections on Policy

Elections determine the leaders who make

decisions on critical national and local policies, including healthcare, education, taxes, civil rights, and foreign relations. The outcomes of elections, especially at the federal level, affect every aspect of life. By understanding the system, voters can grasp the importance of electing representatives who align with their values and interests, ensuring that the government reflects the will of the people.

3. Navigating the Electoral College and its Implications

The unique nature of the Electoral College in U.S. presidential elections can lead to outcomes where the popular vote winner does not win the presidency, as happened in the 2000 and 2016 elections. Understanding how the Electoral College works helps voters recognize the importance of state-by-state voting patterns, especially in swing states, and why these states receive outsized attention during campaigns. This knowledge also informs discussions on potential reforms and whether the Electoral College remains a fair representation of democracy.

4. Preventing Voter Suppression and Encouraging Equity

Awareness of voter suppression tactics, such as

strict voter ID laws, gerrymandering, or the closure of polling places, is essential to safeguard voting rights, particularly for marginalized communities. Understanding the election system equips voters to recognize when such tactics are being used and to advocate for fairer policies. For instance, knowing about the Voting Rights Act of 1965 and its significance in combating discrimination can motivate citizens to protect these hard-won rights.

5. Participation Beyond Presidential Elections

Understanding that the U.S. election system includes various types of elections—local, state, congressional, and judicial—encourages participation beyond just presidential elections. Local and state elections often have more immediate and direct impacts on citizens' day-to-day lives, influencing everything from public schooling to law enforcement practices. Knowledge of the primary elections, midterms, and other electoral processes is vital for citizens who want to have a voice in their governance at all levels.

6. The Role of Campaign Finance and Political Influence

By understanding how campaign finance works, including the role of PACs and Super PACs, voters can critically assess the influence of money in politics. This awareness can drive calls for reform to reduce the disproportionate impact of wealthy donors and corporate interests on the political process, ensuring that ordinary citizens retain influence over elected officials.

7. Ensuring Accountability and Transparency

Informed citizens are better equipped to hold their elected officials accountable. If voters understand how laws are made, how policies are implemented, and how elections are run, they can more effectively demand transparency and ethical behavior from their representatives. In addition, knowing how elections are certified and monitored, including the role of bodies like the Federal Election Commission (FEC), helps ensure trust in the integrity of election outcomes.

8. Promoting Informed Debates and Political Literacy

In a democratic society, political debates shape public opinion and policy direction. An understanding of the election system ensures that citizens can engage in these debates thoughtfully and constructively. This political literacy fosters a more informed electorate, leading to discussions that are based on facts and an understanding of how political processes function, rather than on misinformation or partisan rhetoric.

9. Historical Context and the Evolution of Democracy

Understanding the election system also involves recognizing the historical context of U.S. democracy. This includes the evolution of voting rights through amendments like the 15th, 19th, and 26th Amendments, which expanded suffrage to African Americans, women, and young adults. Knowledge of historical struggles and reforms encourages citizens to appreciate their rights and remain vigilant in protecting them.

In summary, understanding the U.S. election system is crucial for fostering an engaged and informed citizenry. It empowers individuals to exercise their right to vote effectively, ensures they can hold their representatives accountable, and promotes equity and transparency in the democratic process. With the ongoing challenges of voter suppression, campaign finance, and political polarization, knowledge of the election system is key to sustaining a robust and fair democracy.

APPENDIX 1

Books and Academic Sources:

1.   Kissinger, Henry. *World Order*. Penguin Books, 2015.

•   This book by the former U.S. Secretary of State provides insight into the global political landscape and the role the U.S. plays in maintaining order.

2.   Ikenberry, G. John. *Liberal Leviathan: The Origins, Crisis, and Transformation of the American World Order*. Princeton University Press, 2011.

•   This book focuses on the U.S.'s leading role in building and maintaining the liberal international order after World War II.

3.   Nye, Joseph S. *Soft Power: The Means to Success in World Politics*. PublicAffairs, 2004.

•   A discussion of how U.S. influence extends beyond military power through cultural and diplomatic channels.

4.   Friedman, Thomas L. *The World is Flat: A Brief History of the Twenty-First Century*. Farrar, Straus and Giroux, 2005.

•   Focuses on globalization and the United States' role in the interconnected global economy.

5.   Fukuyama, Francis. *The End of History and the Last Man*. Free Press, 1992.

•   Explores the ideological

influence of the U.S. in promoting democracy and liberal values in the post-Cold War world.

6.   Mearsheimer, John J. *The Tragedy of Great Power Politics*. W.W. Norton & Company, 2001.

•   This book discusses the enduring competitive dynamics among global powers, with the U.S. as the main hegemon.

Articles and Reports:

1.   Council on Foreign Relations (CFR). *The U.S. Role in the World: Background and Analysis*.

•   A comprehensive set of reports that cover different aspects of U.S. foreign policy, its alliances, military engagements, and diplomacy. Available at CFR.org.

2.   National Security Strategy (NSS) of the United States. *National Security Strategies*, 2021.

•   This document outlines the U.S. government's strategic priorities in global politics, including defense, trade, and human rights. Available through official government publications.

3.   Pew Research Center. *America's Global Image Remains More Positive than China's, But Gap is Narrowing* (2023).

•   Research on global public opinion regarding U.S. influence and international perceptions. Available at PewResearch.org.

4.   Chatham House. *The U.S. and Global Governance: Power and Leadership in the 21st Century*.

•   Offers an analysis of the changing role of the U.S. in international governance structures. Available at ChathamHouse.org.

News and Media:

1.   The New York Times and Washington Post.

Regular reporting on U.S. foreign policy decisions, military engagements, trade policies, and U.S. relations with China, Russia, and other global actors.

2.   BBC News. Global coverage of U.S. politics and its impact on international relations. Available at BBC.com.

3.   Foreign Affairs Magazine. *U.S. Foreign Policy and International Relations.*

- Offers articles and essays from experts on American influence in the world. Available at ForeignAffairs.com.

4.   The Economist. Regular analysis and reporting on U.S. global influence, particularly in economic and military domains. Available at Economist.com.

Think Tanks and Policy Institutes:

1.   Brookings Institution. *America's Role in the World.*

- Offers deep insights into U.S. foreign policy strategy, global security, and economic influence. Available at Brookings.edu.

2.   The Center for Strategic and International Studies (CSIS).

- Reports and analyses on U.S. military power, diplomacy, and global challenges like climate change and cybersecurity. Available at CSIS.org.

3.   The RAND Corporation. *America's Military and Economic Influence in the Global Arena.*

- Focuses on defense, security, and the U.S.'s role in shaping global economic policies. Available at RAND.org.

Government Websites and Official Reports:

1.   U.S. Department of State. Reports on U.S. foreign relations, diplomatic initiatives, and strategic

partnerships. Available at State.gov.

2.	U.S. Department of Defense. Updates on U.S. military deployments, defense strategies, and global security initiatives. Available at Defense.gov.

3.	CIA World Factbook. Provides comprehensive data on U.S. foreign relations and global influence in various countries. Available at CIA.gov.

Other Online Resources:

1.	The Diplomat. News and analysis on U.S. involvement in the Indo-Pacific and global diplomacy. Available at TheDiplomat.com.

2.	Al Jazeera. Coverage of U.S. foreign policy, including its interventions and global standing, particularly in the Middle East. Available at AlJazeera.com.

APPENDIX 2

Basic Structure of U.S. Government

- Federal System: The U.S. has a federal system, meaning power is divided between a national (federal) government and state governments.
- Three Branches:
  - Executive Branch: The President and their administration.
  - Legislative Branch: Congress (Senate + House of Representatives).
  - Judicial Branch: The Supreme Court and other courts.

Types of Elections

- Presidential Elections: Held every 4 years to elect the President and Vice President.
- Congressional Elections:
  - Senate: Every 6 years, one-third of the Senate is up for election.
  - House of Representatives: All members are elected every 2 years.
- State & Local Elections: Each state and city has its own elections for governors, mayors, and state legislatures.

Who Can Vote?

- Eligibility: U.S. citizens, 18 years or older, can vote.
- Voter Registration: Citizens must register

before voting in many states.

The Two Major Political Parties

- Democratic Party: Generally considered more liberal.
- Republican Party: Generally considered more conservative.
- Other Parties: There are smaller third parties, but Democrats and Republicans dominate the political landscape.

Presidential Elections: The Electoral College

- Primaries and Caucuses:
  - Before the general election, each party holds primaries or caucuses to choose their nominee for President.
- General Election:
  - Held every 4 years in November.
  - Voters don't directly vote for the President but for electors who represent their state in the Electoral College.
- Electoral College:
  - The U.S. has 538 electors (based on the number of Congress members from each state).
  - A candidate needs 270 electoral votes to win the presidency.
  - Most states use a "winner-takes-all" system: the candidate who wins the most votes in the state gets all of that state's electoral votes.
- Inauguration: The winner is inaugurated as President on January 20 of the following year.

Congressional Elections

- Senate:
  - Each state has 2 senators, elected for 6-year terms. Senators are elected on a rotating basis so that only about one-third are up for election at any time.
- House of Representatives:
  - The number of representatives is based on the state's population (bigger states have more representatives).
  - Elected every 2 years.

Voting Process

- Voting Methods:
  - In-person voting: At polling stations.
  - Absentee/Mail-in Voting: Voters can mail their ballots.
- Election Day: Presidential and Congressional elections are typically held on the first Tuesday after the first Monday in November.

How Votes Are Counted

- Popular Vote: The total number of individual votes cast by citizens.
- Electoral Vote (Presidential Election only): The deciding factor in who becomes President, based on the results in each state.

Challenges and Controversies

- Gerrymandering: Drawing voting district lines to benefit a particular party.
- Voter Suppression: Some practices or laws that make it harder for certain groups to vote.
- Electoral College Criticism: Some argue the system isn't fully democratic, as a candidate can win the presidency without winning the national popular vote.

Key Terms to Remember

- Electoral College: The system used to elect the President.
- Popular Vote: The total number of votes cast by the public.
- Primary Elections: Elections to choose a party's candidate.
- Swing States: States where the outcome can go either way, making them crucial in elections.